DK EYEWITNESS TOP 10 TRAVEL GUIDES

WASHINGTON, D.C.

RON BURKE
& SUSAN BURKE

Left **Lincoln Memorial** Right **State Dining Room, The White House**

LONDON, NEW YORK,
MELBOURNE, MUNICH AND DELHI
www.dk.com

Produced by Sargasso Media Ltd, London

Reproduced by Colourscan, Singapore
Printed and bound in Italy by Graphicom

First American Edition, 2003
04 05 06 07 08 10 9 8 7 6 5 4 3 2 1

Published in the United States by
DK Publishing, Inc., 375 Hudson Street,
New York, New York 10014

Reprinted with revisions 2004

**Copyright 2003, 2004 © Dorling
Kindersley Limited, London**

A Catalogue of Publication record is available
from the Library of Congress

ISBN 0-7894-9186-9

Within each Top 10 list in this book, no
hierarchy of quality or popularity is implied.
All 10 are, in the editor's opinion, of roughly
equal merit.

Contents

Washington, D.C.'s Top 10

**The information in this
DK Eyewitness Top 10 Travel Guide is checked regularly.**
Every effort has been made to ensure that this book is as up-to-date as possible at the time
of going to press. Some details, however, such as telephone numbers, opening hours,
prices, gallery hanging arrangements and travel information are liable to change. The
publishers cannot accept responsibility for any consequences arising from the use of this
book, nor for any material on third party websites, and cannot guarantee that any website
address in this book will be a suitable source of travel information. We value the views and
suggestions of our readers very highly. Please write to:
Publisher, DK Eyewitness Travel Guides,
Dorling Kindersley, 80 Strand, London WC2R 0RL, Great Britain.

 Note: *Following the events of September 11, 2001, heightened security measures
have been in place and some sights may be temporarily closed to the public.*

Left **Renwick Gallery** Center **US Botanic Garden** Right **Iwo Jima Memorial**

Left **Washington Monument** Right **Red Fox Inn, Middleburg**

Key to abbreviations
Adm *admission charge* **Free** *no admission charge* **Dis. access** *disabled access*

3

WASHINGTON, D.C.'S TOP 10

WASHINGTON, D.C.'S TOP 10

🔟 Washington, D.C.'s Highlights

A symbol of democracy the world over and the seat of American government, Washington, D.C. confronts visitors with stirring icons and monuments at every turn. This sparkling self-styled city on the Potomac River is full of marble and light, with beautiful landscaping touches and centuries-old architecture. Built on top of former swampland, Washington was deliberately designed into quadrants, with the US Capitol at its hub. Its many unmissable sights provide unparalleled access to the workings of government, internationally famed museums with priceless exhibits, and the cultural and spiritual foundations of the city and the nation.

1 United States Capitol

The Capitol's design combines ancient tradition and New World innovation, perfectly invoking the spirit of US democracy *(see pp8–11)*.

2 The White House

The most elegant and familiar of all the world's political residences, the White House has witnessed some of the most consequential decisions of modern history *(see pp12–15)*.

3 National Air and Space Museum

Reportedly the most visited museum in the world, and with good reason. The artifacts of one of mankind's greatest quests – flight above and beyond Earth – are rendered even more impressive by the hangarlike architecture *(see pp16–17)*.

4 National Museum of American History

Cleverly combining the "America's attic" approach with contemporary interpretive displays, this museum exhibits artifacts ranging from political campaign buttons to early locomotives *(see pp18–19)*.

10 Mount Vernon
George Washington's estate and mansion is a perfect example of the gentleman-farmer roots of many of America's founders *(see pp32–5)*.

9 Arlington National Cemetery
Four million people each year visit these rolling lawns studded with the headstones of America's war dead. A moving and reflective experience *(see pp30–31)*.

5 National Gallery of Art
The National Gallery's vast collection makes it one of the greatest art museums in the world *(see pp20–23)*.

8 National Zoological Park
Animals from across the world's varied habitats can be seen and learned about at this internationally recognized leader in animal care, breeding of endangered species, and public education *(see pp28–9)*.

6 Library of Congress
The breathtaking interior of the largest library in the world does full justice to its 120 million items, displayed on 530 miles (850 km) of shelves *(see pp24–5)*.

7 National Cathedral
Ancient and modern come together in this "national house of prayer," from the Gothic façade to the Space Window *(see pp26–7)*.

🔟 United States Capitol

From the elevated site that Pierre L'Enfant (see p36) described as "a pedestal waiting for a monument", the dignified Capitol has stood unwavering as the symbol of American democracy throughout its 200-year history. From the legislative session called by President Jefferson in 1803 to approve the Louisiana Purchase through to the House of Representatives' vote in 1998 to impeach President Clinton, these halls have witnessed an often rough-and-tumble democratic process. The Capitol's frescoes and art collection qualify it as a notable museum, but its millions of tourists come, above all, to brush shoulders with history, both remembered and in the making.

Façade

⊘ Timed tickets are distributed on a first-come, first-served basis, one per person, beginning at 8:15am at the East Front entrance.

The Capitol is most inspiring when viewed rising up from the Mall.

- *Independence Mall, between 1st and 3rd Sts and Independence and Constitution Aves*
- *Map R5*
- *202-225-6827*
- *www.aoc.gov/ homepage.htm*
- *Open 9am–4:30pm Mon–Sat*
- *Free*

Top 10 Features

1. Capitol Dome
2. Rotunda
3. Senate Chamber
4. House Chamber
5. Old Senate Chamber
6. National Statuary Hall
7. Brumidi Corridors
8. Hall of Columns
9. Columbus Doors
10. West Front

2 Rotunda
America's first president ascends into the heavens in this 4,664-sq ft (430-sq m) fresco *The Apotheosis of Washington*, lining the interior of the dome *(above)*.

1 Capitol Dome
The central dome *(above)* defines the entire city to people worldwide. It was added, with the Statue of Freedom *(see p11)*, by 1866.

3 Senate Chamber
A semicircle of 100 desks faces the dais in this eminent assembly room *(below)*. Democrats sit to the right, Republicans to the left.

For more sights on Capitol Hill See pp70–73

4 House Chamber
The largest room in the Capitol is used for daily deliberations of the House of Representatives and for joint meetings of the House and Senate.

5 Old Senate Chamber
Used by the Senate from 1810 to 1859, this chamber witnessed debates on the core issues of the development of the United States.

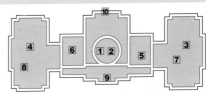

Plan of the US Capitol

9 Columbus Doors
These imposing bronze doors, 17 ft (5 m) tall, consist of reliefs picturing Christopher Columbus's life and his discovery of America. Designed by Randolph Rogers, the doors were cast in Munich in 1860.

10 West Front
The west front of the Capitol *(above)*, facing the Mall, is the site of presidential inaugurations, concerts, and other ceremonial events. Its three-part Neo-Classical façade is an expression of bicameral legislature.

Capitol Guide

Current tours cover the historic sections in the center of the building, including the Rotunda, the National Statuary Hall, and the crypt. The Senate and House galleries are open only when each body is in session. Guided tours are limited to 40 people per group, and leave every half hour from 9:30am to 3:30pm. Entrance for the tour is at the temporary visitor receiving facility, at the southwest end.

6 National Statuary Hall
The monumental *Liberty and the Eagle* by Enrico Causici (c.1819) overlooks this hall *(right)* – the original House Chamber.

7 Brumidi Corridors
Constantino Brumidi (1805–80) designed these ornate passageways *(above)* on the lower floor of the Senate wing.

8 Hall of Columns
This striking corridor, more than 100 ft (30 m) long with lofty ceilings, is named after the 28 gracefully fluted white marble columns along its length. It houses additional items from the collection of the National Statuary Hall.

Left **British burn the Capitol, 1814** Right **Charles Bulfinch**

Events in the US Capitol's History

1 1787
The US Constitution authorizes the establishment of a federal district to be the seat of the American government.

2 1791
George Washington selects the site for the new Capitol, with his city planner, Pierre Charles L'Enfant, on Jenkins Hill, 88 ft (27 m) above the Potomac River.

3 1792
Dr. William Thornton wins a design contest for "Congress House," in which he proposed a simple central domed hall flanked by two rectangular wings.

4 1800
Congress moves from Philadelphia to occupy the north wing of the Capitol.

George Washington

5 1810
The Capitol is fully occupied by the House of Representatives and Senate, the Supreme Court, and Library of Congress.

6 1814
British troops burn the Capitol during the War of 1812.

7 1815
Charles Bulfinch redesigns the fire-damaged building and supervises reconstruction. The Senate and Supreme Court occupy new rooms by 1819 and the Rotunda is first used in 1824 to host a grand reception for General Lafayette.

8 1851
The Capitol is again damaged by fire. It is redesigned and rebuilt once more under the direction of Charles Bulfinch and Thomas U. Walter, who designs the cast-iron dome. Work is interrupted during the Civil War, when the Capitol is used as a hospital, barracks, and bakery.

9 1885–1900
Modern plumbing and electrical lighting are installed for the first time.

10 1958–1962
The east front is completely rebuilt, 32 ft (10 m) east of the old sandstone front. The west front is restored between 1983 and 1987. This work produces the Capitol we see today.

For more moments in Washington, D.C.'s history **See pp36–7**

The Statue of Freedom

Crowning the Capitol dome stands Thomas Crawford's Statue of Freedom, and, according to Capitol police guards, the figure is the most common subject of visitors' questions. Why does it face to the east, away from the nation? Freedom is depicted as a classical female figure, draped in flowing robes. Her Roman helmet, however, features the crest of an eagle's head, feathers, and talons, which some believe to be a reference to Native American dress. Crawford substituted the Roman helmet for the original liberty cap, a symbol of freed slaves, when the then US Secretary of War, Jefferson Davis, objected. The statue faces east in accordance with the front of the building, not the rest of the country. The east front was made the main building entrance simply because it faces an approach of level ground. This monumental symbol of liberty is 19.5 ft (6 m) tall and weighs around 15,000 lbs (6,800 kg).

The American Ideal

Although the Statue of Freedom may appear to face away from the heartland, she is, nevertheless, the embodiment of all Americans. Standing imperiously over the capital, and the nation as a whole, she encapsulates the notion of freedom for all citizens, laid out in the US Constitution. It is an ideal still fiercely protected today.

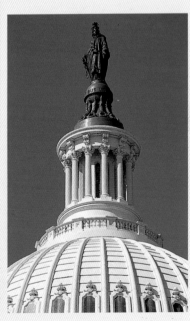

🔟 The White House

Possibly the most famous residential landmark in the world, this dramatic Neo-Classical mansion has been the residence of the US president and family, the seat of executive power, and a working office building for over 200 years. Situated at the nation's most recognizable address, 1600 Pennsylvania Avenue, the White House reflects the power of the presidency. Its 132 rooms preserve and display the cultural settings of America's past and present. Lafayette Park to the north and the Ellipse to the south are popular sites for viewing this American icon.

North façade

🔁 If you have a tele-photo lens or binoculars, the carved floral decorations on the north entrance and the plantings of the Rose Garden, viewed from the Ellipse, deserve attention.

The White House has no public restrooms. The nearest facilities are at the Visitor Center and the Ellipse Visitor Pavilion, near 15th and E streets NW.

• 1600 Pennsylvania Ave, NW (Visitor Center: Dept of Commerce, 14th & 15th Sts on Pennsylvania Ave, NW)
• Map N4
• 202-208-1631
• www.nps.gov/whho
• Current information about tours can be obtained at 202-456-7041
• Free
• Dis. access

Top 10 Features

1 North Façade
2 South Façade
3 Oval Office
4 West Wing
5 East Room
6 Blue Room
7 Map Room
8 State Dining Room
9 Lincoln Bedroom
10 Visitor Center

1 North Façade
The stately but welcoming main entrance on Pennsylvania Avenue has a beautifully propor-tioned Ionic portico, added in 1829. Painted Virginia sandstone gives the building its white luster.

2 South Façade
The large semi-circular portico added in 1824 dominates the south view. The six main columns create an optical illusion, appearing to stretch from ground to roofline, emphasizing the classical proportions.

3 Oval Office
This illustrious room *(above)* is the setting for the president's core tasks. Each leader adds his own touches – George W Bush has deco-rated it with paintings of his native Texas by Texan artists.

4 West Wing
This wing is the executive operational center of the White House, moved here in 1902 to allow more privacy in the main building.

5 East Room
The East Room *(left)* has been used chiefly for large entertainment or ceremonial gatherings, such as dances, award presenta-tions, press conferences, and historic bill signings.

For more sights around the White House **See pp90–93**

Blue Room
6 The Blue Room *(above)* is the most elegant of all the reception rooms – it was George Washington who suggested its oval shape.

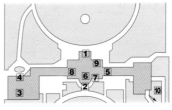

Plan of the White House

Visitor Center
10 The White House Visitor Center *(above)* has engrossing exhibits on various aspects of the mansion. It also offers park ranger talks, a souvenir shop, and special events such as military band concerts.

Map Room
7 Graceful Chippendale furniture features in this private meeting room. Franklin D. Roosevelt adapted it as his situation room to assess the progress of World War II.

State Dining Room
8 As many as 140 guests may enjoy the president's hospitality in this formal dining room *(below)*.

Lincoln Bedroom
9 Although the name for this room is a misnomer – Abraham Lincoln used it as an office – a number of his possessions can be found here. Mary Todd Lincoln bought the imposing Victorian bed *(above)*, made of carved rosewood, in 1861.

Designing the White House

George Washington personally supervised the design and construction of the White House, although he never lived here. John and Abigail Adams became its first residents in 1800. At the same time, the seat of government was moved from Philadelphia to Washington, D.C. After the British burned the White House in 1814, it became the responsibility of the James Monroe presidency to redecorate. Much of what is seen today reflects Monroe's taste.

Left **Vermeil Room** Right **Diplomatic Reception Room**

White House Decorative Features

1 The Vermeil Room
"Vermeil" refers to the collection of gilded objects by early 19th-century silversmiths on display. Delightful portraits of seven First Ladies adorn the walls, and the room is grounded by an exquisite Empire-style mahogany table in the center.

2 China Room Collection
The White House collection of china services had grown so large by 1917 that Mrs. Woodrow Wilson set aside a special room in which to display it. State and family china belonging to nearly every US president fills the fine display cabinets.

3 Grand Staircase
Descending gracefully to the Central Hall on the north side, the Grand Staircase is used for ceremonial entrances to state events in the East Room. Portraits of 20th-century presidents line the stairwell.

4 Library
This former storage room was turned into a library in 1935, and contains a collection of books intended to reflect the philosophical and practical aspects of the presidency. The furniture is attributed to the cabinetmaker Duncan Phyfe.

5 Diplomatic Reception Room Wallpaper
The panoramic wallpaper in this room is a series of large "Views of North America" printed in 1834.

6 Lighter Relieving a Steamboat Aground
This 1847 painting in the Green Room, by George Caleb Bingham, conveys the vitality of the nation.

7 Sand Dunes at Sunset, Atlantic City
This beach landscape (c.1885) by Henry Ossawa Tanner was the first work by an African-American to be hung in the White House.

8 North Entrance Carvings
Scottish stonemasons created the carved surround for the north doorway with flowing garlands of roses and acorns.

9 Monroe Plateau
James Monroe brought a gilt table service from France in 1817. The plateau centerpiece is an impressive 14.5 ft (4.5 m) long when fully extended.

10 Seymour Tall-Case Clock
This Oval Office clock ticks so loudly that its pendulum must be stopped when television broadcasts originate from the room.

Grand Staircase

Top 10 Events in The White House's History

President Truman's Renovations

From the time Harry S. Truman moved into the White House, he had noticed signs that the building was under a great deal of stress: "The floors pop and the drapes move back and forth," and "[t]he damned place is haunted, sure as shootin'." In 1948, after some investigation, engineers confirmed that it was structural weakness, not ghosts, that was causing the problems. Some people said the house was standing "only from force of habit." The only certain solution was to move the Truman family to nearby Blair House and completely rebuild the White House within its external walls. Contractors gutted the inside of the building in its entirety – every floor, wall, ceiling, closet, pipe, wire, and fixture came out. Workers then built a steel frame, similar to those found in large office buildings, inside the remaining shell. Within the frame, the White House was recreated, room by room, from scratch, but in keeping with the original design. Everything structural that can be seen today in the house was built between 1948 and 1952. America's three major networks broadcast the first-ever television tour of the residence in 1952. President Truman himself proudly led the tour and even entertained viewers by playing a tune on one of the pianos in the East Room (see p12). A decade later, that arbiter of style Jacqueline Kennedy again restored many of the period features.

The White House gutted in 1948

ⓉⓄₚ10 National Air and Space Museum

This fascinating museum's 23 main exhibition galleries pay homage to some of the most ingenious and beautifully crafted objects of flight, from the Wright brothers' airplane, steered by bending its flexible frame, to the complex and powerful ships that carried humans into space. Compelling exhibitions put these historic objects in the context of their social and political settings. Another highlight is the moon rock, displayed so that the public can touch it.

Museum façade

🍴 McDonald's, Boston Market, and Donato's Pizzeria are located in the greenhouse-like extension on the east end of the building.

🎁 The gift shop displays the model of the USS *Enterprise* used in the filming of *Star Trek*. This is the largest of the Smithsonian shops and worth a visit (see p82).

• Independence Ave, SW & 7th St, SW
• Map Q5
• 202-357-2700
• www.nasm.si.edu
• Open 10am–5:30pm daily; closed Dec 25
• Dis. access
• Museum: Free; Planetarium shows: $4.00; Lockheed Martin IMAX Theater: $6.50; Theater/Planetarium Combo: $9.00
• Steven F. Udvar-Hazy Center: Dulles International Airport; Opening Dec 2003

Top 10 Exhibits

1 1903 Wright *Flyer*
2 Ryan NYP *Spirit of St. Louis*
3 Apollo 11 Command Module *Columbia*
4 Amelia Earhart's Lockheed Vega
5 Skylab Orbital Workshop
6 How Things Fly
7 Looking at Earth
8 Re-enactment of the *Eagle* Moon Landing
9 World War I Aviation
10 Steven F. Udvar-Hazy Center

Independen Avenue entrance

1903 Wright Flyer
On December 17, 1903, Orville Wright flew this craft *(above)* 120 ft (35 m), making it the first plane to be air-borne. Muslin fitted with a spruce and ash framework provided a light but strong body. The Wright brothers also designed the engine.

Apollo 11 Command Module Columbia
This vessel was the command center for the first human landing in space, photographing the moon and carrying Neil Armstrong and "Buzz" Aldrin back to Earth.

Ryan NYP Spirit of St. Louis
Charles A. Lindbergh flew this plane *(below)* on the first transatlantic flight, 3,610 miles (5,810 km) from Long Island to Paris in 1927. His 33-hour solo flight made him one of the most famous men of his age and turned aviation into a public craze. NYP stands for New York–Paris.

For more museums in Washington, D.C. See pp42–3

4 Amelia Earhart's Lockheed 5B Vega

In this striking airplane *(above)*, Amelia Earhart completed the second solo nonstop flight across the Atlantic, from Newfoundland to Ireland in 14 hours, 54 minutes.

5 Skylab Orbital Workshop

This gold cylinder *(below)* was an identical backup to the workshop that provided living and research space for the first US space station.

6 How Things Fly

Hands-on exhibits here lead visitors through the basics of flight, both human and animal, and explain forces that control flight of all types, from a helium balloon to a mission to Mars.

7 Looking at Earth

The focus here is on the contribution aerial photography *(below)* and space flight have given to our understanding of Earth. Also memorable is the breathtaking beauty of some of the images.

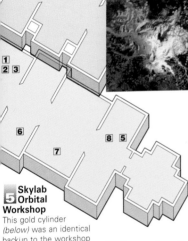

8 Re-enactment of the Eagle Moon Landing

Much of the world held its breath on July 20, 1969, as Neil Armstrong and "Buzz" Aldrin and the Lunar Module *Eagle* approached and touched down on the moon's Sea of Tranquillity. Visitors can re-experience one of the 20th century's most thrilling moments in this multimedia display.

9 World War I Aviation

Fokker, SPAD, Sopwith, and other aircraft *(below)* of the Great War evoke visions of almost courtly air battles, but the realities of the era's air power explained here help dispel the nostalgia.

10 Steven F. Udvar-Hazy Center

This new aviation area at Dulles International Airport is an extension of the museum, and will consist of two exhibition hangars, one over 100 ft (30 m) high. It will allow NASM to display over 300 extra aircraft and spacecraft. Scheduled to open in December 2003.

Key

First Floor

Second Floor

Museum Guide

Entrances to the museum are on both Independence Avenue and the Mall. Both lead into the spacious central hall where the most famous airplanes of all time are displayed overhead. An information booth is near the Independence Avenue entrance. Visitors who plan to enjoy a film at the Lockheed Martin IMAX Theater or the Albert Einstein Planetarium should obtain their tickets on arrival, since seats are often not available immediately.

TOP 10 National Museum of American History

Three huge floors filled with a variety of fascinating objects make up this paean to American culture. The first floor focuses on science and technology: tools of the Industrial Revolution are here, as well as locomotives, farm equipment, old automobiles, and objects of the 20th-century information age. Mementos of American cultural history, including immigration, internal migration, and the role of women, fill the second floor. The third floor features a stirring tribute to the American presidency.

Façade

The period ice cream parlor (directly in front of the Constitution Avenue entrance) captures the feel of an earlier era in its decor, service, and delicious desserts.

- 14th St and Constitution Ave, NW
- Map P4
- 202-357-2700
- www.americanhistory. si.edu/
- Open 10am–5:30pm daily; closed Dec 25
- Dis. access
- Free

Top 10 Exhibits

1. The Star-Spangled Banner
2. Within These Walls
3. Fast Attacks and Boomers
4. First Ladies' Hall
5. Information Age
6. 1967 Pontiac Grand Prix Convertible
7. Communities in a Changing Nation
8. Sitting for Justice
9. The American Presidency
10. Hands-On History Room

1 The Star-Spangled Banner

The flag that inspired the national anthem is strikingly large – originally 30 by 42 ft (9 by 13 m) – but sadly worn. Created by Baltimore flagmaker Mary Pickersgill in 1813, it is being painstakingly repaired in a preservation laboratory, which is open to public view *(below)*.

2 Within These Walls

A two-story colonial house from Massachusetts has been rebuilt within the museum, to explore the 200-year history of the families who lived there *(below)*.

3 Fast Attacks and Boomers

An intriguing interactive, walk-through look at these consummate Cold War tools. Fast attacks are 360-ft (110-m) nuclear submarines designed to find and track enemy subs. Boomers are ballistic missile subs, 560 ft (170 m) long.

For moments in the history of Washington, D.C. See pp36–7

Key

▦	First Floor
▦	Second Floor
▦	Third Floor

6 1967 Pontiac Grand Prix Convertible
In the 1960s Americans were devoting more time to leisure, and sports cars became popular. The Grand Prix typified the era with its sleek shape.

7 Communities in a Changing Nation
This exhibit explores the ever-changing world of 19th-century America, revealing the everyday experiences of workers in new factories, of Jewish immigrants, and of enslaved and free African Americans.

4 First Ladies' Hall
The First Ladies' gown gallery *(above)* has long been a favorite exhibit. In dim lighting to protect the fabrics, visitors experience a voyage back in time through changing women's fashions.

5 Information Age
Telegraph, telephone, radio, television, computers: this thread of technological development is key to the shape of contemporary life. From Samuel Morse to Seymour Cray, the entire story is here *(right)*.

8 Sitting for Justice
On February 1, 1960, four African-American students in Greensboro, North Carolina, sat at this lunch counter of the Woolworth store and tried to order food. When they were told to leave, their "passive sit-down demand" energized a powerful movement challenging the segregationist laws of the southern states.

9 The American Presidency
The portable desk Thomas Jefferson used to write the Declaration of Independence and the hat Abraham Lincoln was wearing the night he was assassinated are highlights of this history of the presidential office.

10 Hands-On History Room
Visitors here can use outdated technology, such as sending a telegraph message, pedaling a high-wheel bicycle, and hand-turning a cotton gin *(above)*.

Museum Events
An amazing quantity and variety of events, both entertaining and enlightening, are available to the public at the museum. A tiny sampling includes demonstrations of quilt-making, special tours of the history and conservation of the Star-Spangled Banner, performances by the Axelrod String Quartet on instruments built by Stradivari and his teacher, Amati, and a symposium on African-American genealogy in the 21st century. Some events require reservations, and a few require tickets.

Washington, D.C.'s Top 10

🔟 National Gallery of Art

The collections at this immense gallery rival those of any art museum in the world, displaying milestones of western art from the Middle Ages through to the 20th century, including Italian Renaissance works, Dutch Masters, French Impressionists, and all ages of American art. John Russell Pope designed the harmonious Neo-Classical West Building in 1941. The newer East Building is the work of architect IM Pei and it is often considered a work of art in itself.

East Building

🍴 The Cascade Café, on the concourse between the West and East Buildings, has an espresso bar with ice cream, sandwiches, and other treats.

🌿 The East Garden Court on the main floor is a wonderful place to relax, away from the constant stream of tourists.

• 3rd–9th Sts at Constitution Avenue NW
• Map Q4
• 202-737-4215
• www.nga.gov/
• Open 10am–5pm Mon–Sat, 11am–6pm Sun; closed Dec 25, Jan 1
• Free
• Dis. access

Top 10 Paintings

1. Ginevra de' Benci
2. The Adoration of the Magi
3. Girl with the Red Hat
4. The Alba Madonna
5. Watson and the Shark
6. Portraits of the First Five Presidents
7. Wivenhoe Park, Essex
8. Symphony in White, No. 1: The White Girl
9. Woman with a Parasol – Madame Monet and Her Son
10. Number 1, 1950 (Lavender Mist)

1 Ginevra de' Benci
The careful modeling of the face and the contrast of lustrous flesh with juniper foliage make this Leonardo da Vinci 1474 portrait a lively but composed work *(above)*.

2 The Adoration of the Magi
This festive view of the Magi at Christ's birthplace *(right)* was painted in tempera on a circular panel by Fra Angelico and Filippo Lippi in about 1445.

3 Girl with the Red Hat
This 1665 portrait *(above)* shows off Johannes Vermeer's striking use of color: yellow highlights in the blue robe, purple under the hat, turquoise in the eyes. The luminosity is enhanced by the smooth panel base.

4 The Alba Madonna

Unusually, the Madonna in Raphael's 1510 work is shown seated on the ground. The composition is serene, but it shows Christ accepting the cross from St John the Baptist, a precursor of events to come.

5 Watson and the Shark

The sensational subject matter, muscular painting, and expressions of dread and anxiety made this John Singleton Copley painting shocking when it was first displayed in 1778.

7 Wivenhoe Park, Essex

Light and shade, the perception of calm, and clarity of detail create an absorbing and soothing landscape *(above)*. In this 1816 work John Constable demonstrates his love of the English countryside.

8 Symphony in White, No. 1: The White Girl

This 1862 work by James McNeill Whistler *(right)* is a precursor of Modernism, emphasizing abstract forms over the sensuous recreation of the model, the artist's mistress, Joanna Heffernan.

9 Woman with a Parasol – Madame Monet and Her Son

The human figures are part of nature here, fully integrated with the landscape. Curators believe this 1875 Claude Monet portrait was painted in a single session.

Constitution Avenue entrance

East Building

10 Number 1, 1950 (Lavender Mist)

This Jackson Pollock composition is a monument of America's emergence as a center of art innovation (1950).

6 Portraits of the First Five Presidents

This is the only complete set of Gilbert Stuart's paintings of the first five presidents (1817–21), including George Washington *(right)*, still in existence. Sadly another set was partially destroyed by fire in 1851 at the Library of Congress.

Gallery Guide

The first floor contains European paintings and sculpture through the 19th century, American art, and temporary exhibitions. The ground floor has displays of works on paper, decorative arts, and temporary exhibits. An underground concourse leads to the East Building.

Left **Salem Cove**, Prendergast Center **Japanese Footbridge**, Monet Right **The East Building**

National Gallery of Art Collections

1 American Paintings

Collections Floorplan

The breadth of this collection reveals many themes: portraiture, a desire for accuracy in depicting American life and landscape (see *Salem Cove*, above), and a social conscience.

2 French 19th-century Paintings

Especially rich in works of the Impressionists, this collection includes some of the world's most beloved works of art, such as Monet's *Japanese Footbridge*. Manet and Degas also feature.

3 Italian 15th-century Paintings

Best known for the increasing mastery of the naturalistic portrayal of the human figure and of interior and exterior

Portrait of an Elderly Lady, Frans Hals

settings, the works in this collection still have appealing variety: decorative, mystical, simple, and elegant.

4 Italian 16th-century Painting

The mature flowering of the Renaissance bursts forth in this deep and broad collection of works by Raphael, Giorgione, Titian, and many others.

5 Works on Paper

The National Gallery is especially strong in this area. Repeat visitors see an almost unbelievable quantity and variety of exquisite drawings, prints, illustrated books, and photographs. The permanent collection contains more than 65,000 items, dating as far back as the 11th century.

6 Dutch and Flemish Paintings

Again, visitors will find an overwhelmingly rich array of Old Master works by artists such as Rembrandt, Frans Hals, Van Dyck, Rubens, Vermeer, and their contemporaries.

7 Spanish Paintings

El Greco, Zurbarán, Murillo, and Velázquez are just some of the Spanish highlights in this vibrant collection.

Constitution Avenue entrance

Mall entrance

Second Floor

First Floor

For more art galleries in Washington, D.C. **See pp40–41**

8 Decorative Arts

Sumptuous tapestries, full of imagery, outstanding pieces of furniture, and everyday items such as plates and bowls, give a wonderful glimpse of the passing centuries in Europe.

9 European Sculpture

Portrait busts and portrait medals have always been important products of the sculptor's studio, and many fine examples are displayed here. There is also an especially absorbing look at Rodin and some experimental sculptural pieces by Degas.

10 Painting and Sculpture of the 20th Century

The frantic rate of change in 20th-century art is laid out here. From Matisse's Fauvist works, the Cubists Picasso and Braque, the abstraction of Mondrian, Surrealists such as Magritte and Miró, high Modernists David Smith, and Mark Rothko, right up to minimalism and Pop Art.

Top 10 Works in the Sculpture Garden

1. *Puellae (Girls)*, Magdalena Abakanowicz (1992)
2. *House I*, Roy Lichtenstein (1996–8)
3. *Four-Sided Pyramid*, Sol LeWitt (1997)
4. *Cheval Rouge*, Alexander Calder (1974)
5. *Personnage Gothique, Oiseau-Éclair*, Joan Miró (1974)
6. *Six-Part Seating*, Scott Burton (1985–98)
7. *Spider*, Louise Bourgeois (1996)
8. *Thinker on a Rock*, Barry Flanagan (1997)
9. *Chair Transformation Number 20B*, Lucas Samaras (1996)
10. *Moondog*, Tony Smith (1964–99)

The East Building and Sculpture Garden

The East Building is an angular construction designed specifically to house permanent and touring exhibitions of contemporary art. Its entrance is from 4th Street or from the underground concourse leading from the West Building. The huge orange-and-black mobile by Alexander Calder that dominates the lobby was reconditioned recently to restore its slow motion. Provocative exhibition halls line the outer walls of the upper halls, connected by spectacular hanging crosswalks. Landscape architect Laurie D. Olin and the National Gallery curators created the Sculpture Garden, a wonderful, lively public space integrated with the display of contemporary art, beautifully landscaped around its fountain and reflecting pool. The pool is turned into an ice skating rink in winter.

Cheval Rouge
This striking work by sculptor Alexander Calder was crafted in 1974. Its depiction of a "red horse" is a perfect example of the abstraction used by modern sculptors.

🖼 Library of Congress

The focus of this immense library – the greatest accumulation of information and images in the world – is the magnificent Jefferson Building. Its main reading room is one of the most captivating spaces in the city, gleaming with its recently refurbished decorations. Collections encompass many subjects – the law library is especially notable, as are materials and books relating to Africa, the Middle East, and the rest of the world. In addition there are collections of comic books, jazz recordings and memorabilia, photography, films, and television broadcasts.

Façade

🕐 Free tickets are often available for concerts beginning at 6:30pm for 8pm performances and 12:30pm for 2pm performances.

For visitors wishing to use the library for research, reader cards can be obtained on the same day by applying at Room LM 401 in the Madison Building.

• 1st St, SE, between Independence Ave and E Capitol St
• Map S5
• 202-707-5000
• www.loc.gov
• Open 10am–5:30pm Mon–Sat; tours: 10:30am, 11:30am, 1:30pm, 2:30pm, 3:30pm Mon–Fri; 10:30am, 11:30am, 1:30pm, 2:30pm Sat
• Dis. access
• Free

Top 10 Features

1. Exterior
2. Main Reading Room
3. Great Hall
4. Gutenberg Bible
5. American Treasures Exhibit
6. African and Middle Eastern Reading Room
7. Mosaic of Minerva
8. Concert Series
9. Film Series
10. Neptune Fountain

1 Exterior
Congress authorized the construction of a new library building in the style of the Italian Renaissance in 1886. Its plan reflects that of the Capitol – two wings with a central dome. The portico contains busts of nine "great men of literature" from Demosthenes to Washington Irving.

2 Main Reading Room
In this splendid room *(above)* the civilized arts are represented by allegorical figures atop its eight giant columns: Religion, History, Commerce, Art, Philosophy, Poetry, Law, and Science.

3 Great Hall
The ceiling, resplendent with stained-glass skylights, soars 75 ft (20 m) above the beautiful marble floor. Ceremonial staircases *(left)* at either end of the hall are elaborately carved with scenes of cherubs engaged in making music, catching butterflies, and using the newly invented telephone.

Gutenberg Bible 4

This superb example of the first book printed with movable type *(right)* is one of only three perfect vellum copies to survive. Also here is the handwritten Giant Bible of Mainz.

Key

First Floor

Second Floor

Third Floor

Mosaic of Minerva 7

A beautiful marble mosaic of Minerva overlooks the staircase near the Visitors' Gallery *(below)*.

Library of Congress Floorplan

Neptune Fountain 10

Roland Hinton Perry sculpted this dashing tribute to the god Neptune and his court *(above)*, installed in 1898 in front of the Jefferson Building.

Jefferson's Collection

The library had humble beginnings of just 3,000 books, but these were destroyed when the British burned the Capitol building, then home to the library, in 1814. Congress appropriated $23,950 to buy Thomas Jefferson's personal library of 6,487 volumes as the core of a new collection. Another fire in 1851 destroyed many of the books. It has been a goal of the library to replace Jefferson's books with period copies, and today only 900 are still missing.

American Treasures Exhibit 5

At any given time historical gems are on display here. Along with Thomas Jefferson's draft of the Declaration of Independence, typical items are atlases of early America, and objects from the mourning of the death of Abraham Lincoln.

African and Middle Eastern Reading Room 6

This long room, for research work on this ancient geographical area, is one of 10 that give users access to the special collections.

Concert Series 8

This distinguished series presents a range of performances: classical song, harpsichord, solo, trio, and quartet programs, period instrument ensembles, jazz, spirituals, and gospel. Concerts are free.

Film Series 9

Classic films are shown in an intimate setting several times a week. Miniseries on subjects such as jazz or Russian cinema run concurrently with the main series.

🔟 Washington National Cathedral

This glorious Gothic building is the focus of public spiritual life for the city and the nation. The structure – the sixth largest cathedral in the world – was completed in 1990, with a 10-story-high nave and a central tower 676 ft (206 m) above sea level, the highest point in the District of Columbia. Officially named the Cathedral Church of Saint Peter and Saint Paul, the church is Episcopal but invites people of all faiths to worship.

Exterior

⭐ The Cathedral Center for Prayer and Pilgrimage is a carpeted room on the lower level, provided for prayer and meditation. Pillows on the floor and subdued candlelight create a tranquil atmosphere.

Binoculars or a telephoto lens are a must for appreciating the gargoyles.

- Massachusetts & Wisconsin Aves NW
- Map H4
- 202-537-6200
- www.nationalcathedral.org
- Open 10am–5:30pm Mon–Fri, 10am–4pm Sat, 12:30–4pm Sun
- Donation
- Dis. access

Top 10 Features

1. Exterior
2. Main Entrance and Creation
3. High Altar
4. Space Window
5. Nave
6. South Rose Window
7. Children's Chapel
8. Gargoyles
9. Pipe Organ
10. Gardens

1 Exterior

The architecture of the cathedral is predominantly English Gothic, created using authentic methods preserved since the Middle Ages, including a cross-shaped floorplan, flying buttresses, and multispired towers.

2 Main Entrance and Creation

The west entrance *(above)* is centered within a high Gothic arch containing a lovely rose window. Above the bronze double doors is *"Ex Nihilo,"* a relief sculpture by Frederick Hart portraying the creation of humankind from chaos.

3 High Altar

The imposing high altar at the east end of the nave *(below)* is made from stone dug from Solomon's quarry outside Jerusalem; the altar is also called the Jerusalem Altar.

Space Window

This stained-glass window **4** is notable for commemorating mankind's 20th-century leap into space *(right)*. A piece of moon rock, brought back by Apollo 11, is embedded in the window.

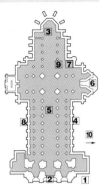

Children's Chapel

7 This endearing room is child-scaled with a miniature organ and altar and chairs to fit six-year-olds. Jesus is also shown as a boy in the sculpture here *(below)*.

Cathedral Floorplan

Gardens

10 A medieval walled garden is the model for the cathedral's beautiful Bishop's Garden on the south side of the church. The herb gardens are a delight to the nose as well as the eye: all the stones here originated in a quarry that George Washington once owned.

Gargoyles

8 Derived from decorated spouts on European buildings, these carved ornaments have been given almost free rein at the cathedral. The 112 grotesque carvings include Darth Vader of *Star Wars*® fame and a predatory-looking owl.

Nave

5 The horizontal impression given by the nave *(above)* is also typical of English Gothic style. Flags of the states are displayed around the outer walls.

Pipe Organ

9 This magnificent Aeolian-Skinner instrument has 10,650 pipes. On Wednesdays at 12:45pm, an organist gives a presentation and then demonstrates with a stirring recital.

South Rose Window

6 "The Church Triumphant" is the theme of this elegant stained-glass window *(right)*. The design of Rowan LeCompte incorporates 12 brilliantly colored vignettes and numerous other figures.

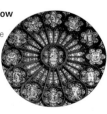

Building the Cathedral

In 1893 Congress granted a charter to construct Washington National Cathedral. Theodore Roosevelt attended the laying of the foundation stone at the commanding Mount St. Albans location in 1907. The completion of the west towers in 1990 marked the end of 83 years of continuous work. The cathedral is built by the "stone-on-stone" method, using no structural steel. Many architects, including Henry Vaughan, Philip Frohman, and George Bodley, came together to create this inspiring monument. It was built entirely from donations.

₁₀ National Zoological Park

One of the most visited destinations in Washington, the National Zoo is a beautifully landscaped 163-acre urban park as well as an innovative center for animal care and conservation. Children and adults delight at seeing rare giant pandas, a playful Asian elephant calf, or a Sumatran tiger cub. More than 3,500 animals live here, increasingly housed in habitats that allow more natural behavior. The zoo, which opened in 1889, was the first in the world to be founded partly with the goal of preserving endangered species.

Entrance sign

🐾 Most children's tour groups arrive between 10am and noon in the fall. If you wish to see the popular giant pandas, visit after 2pm when the lines are shorter.

- 3001 Connecticut Ave, NW
- Map J4
- 202-673-4800/4950
- www.natzoo.si.edu/
- Open May–Sep 15: grounds 6am–8pm, buildings 10am–6pm daily; Sep 16–Apr: grounds 6am–6pm, buildings 10am–4:30pm daily
- Dis. access
- Free

Top 10 Features

1. Giant Pandas
2. Sumatran Tigers
3. Elephant House
4. Bird House and Flight Exhibit
5. Golden Lion Tamarins
6. Think Tank
7. American Prairie
8. Beaver Valley
9. Komodo Dragons
10. Great Ape House

1 Giant Pandas

Mei Xiang and Tian Tian, two giant pandas from China, made their first public appearance at the zoo in January 2001. Their lively curiosity, social interactions, and physical beauty fascinate everyone who sees these wonderful creatures.

2 Sumatran Tigers

This extremely endangered species has been successfully bred at the National Zoo. Estimates put the population of these dark, striped beauties *(below)* at less than 500 in the wild and 170 in zoos.

3 Elephant House

Asian elephants *(below)*, hippos, giraffes, and the greater one-horned rhino are free to roam here. Viewpoints are close enough to appreciate their great size.

4 Bird House and Flight Exhibit

Here, numerous species of birds display their spectacular colors and elegant motions. The flight exhibit is a netted structure *(above)* that gives even birds of prey enough headroom to show off.

5 Golden Lion Tamarins

In summer, these squirrel-sized primates run free in the trees around Valley Trail. These Brazilian animals have been the subject of one of the most successful conservation efforts.

6 Think Tank

Orangutans are taking part in a long-term study of their cognitive and language abilities in this large building. Visitors can watch researchers investigate the animals' use of symbols.

8 Beaver Valley

Beavers share their valley with other North American wildlife, including gray seals *(right)*, California sea lions, hawks, river otters, and Mexican wolves.

Rock Creek Park entrance

Main entrance

National Zoological Park Plan

10 Great Ape House

Western lowland gorillas *(below)* are among our closest relatives, sharing about 98 percent common genome. Their deliberate movements and human-like manner mesmerize observers.

9 Komodo Dragons

These lizards *(below)* can grow as large as 200 lbs (90 kg) and 10 ft (3 m) long. The zoo has been important in preserving these predators; in 1992, 13 dragons hatched here, the first born outside their native Indonesia.

Zoo Horticulture

The zoo is a lush park for both human visitors and its animal residents. Satisfying both presents challenges for the zoo horticulturists. The Great Prairie exhibit, for example, uses over 110 different types of plants to re-create the lost expanses of the Great Plains, while cheetahs wander around a re-creation of the grasslands of their native African habitat.

7 American Prairie

This popular exhibit recalls America's fabled western grasslands through the re-creation of their complex eco-system *(above)*. Broad-shouldered bison graze while prairie dogs cavort like cartoon characters.

The Cleveland Park metro stop is most convenient for the Connecticut Avenue entrance, avoiding an uphill walk.

29

⑩ Arlington National Cemetery

Some of America's most cherished burial sites are found in the 612 acres of the nation's best-known military cemetery. The rolling lawns filled with white tombstones, the Tomb of the Unknowns, and the grave of John F Kennedy are conspicuous symbols of sacrifices made for freedom. The flags fly at half-staff from before the first and after the last of about 20 funerals per day, as the graves of veterans continue to multiply. Nearly four million people visit the cemetery every year, some attracted by the historical importance of the site, many wishing to honor those who have died in the nation's wars, others taking part in the funeral of a friend or family member. The cemetery visitors' center provides maps, personalized information, and guidance.

Arlington House

⊙ Covering the cemetery on foot requires walking long distances. The most convenient way to get to the cemetery is to take the Tourmobile from any of its 25 stops *(see p117)*. They offer a cemetery-only tour that provides transportation through the cemetery along with commentary and interpretation.

- Arlington, VA
- Map K6
- 703-697-9486
- www.arlington cemetery.org
- Open Apr–Sep: 8am–7pm daily; Oct–Mar: 8am–5pm daily
- Free
- Dis. access

Top 10 Features

1. Lawns of Graves
2. Tomb of the Unknowns
3. Memorial Amphitheater
4. Arlington House
5. Confederate Memorial
6. Grave of John F Kennedy
7. Tomb of Pierre L'Enfant
8. Seabees Memorial
9. Challenger Shuttle Memorial
10. Rough Riders Memorial

1 Lawns of Graves

More than 280,000 people are buried on these grounds, marked by unadorned graves, arranged in regular grids, spread across the lawns *(right)*. Although only a small percentage of America's war dead lie here, the expanse gives a tangible picture of the human cost of war.

2 Tomb of the Unknowns

This solemn monument *(right)* is guarded 24 hours a day by The Old Guard. Unknown soldiers of World Wars I and II and the Korean War are entombed here. A Vietnam soldier was interred here, but he was later identified.

3 Memorial Amphitheater

The setting for the Memorial Day and Veterans Day ceremonies *(see p65)*.

4 Arlington House

This impressive mansion was conceived as a memorial to George Washington, built by his step-grandson.

For more memorials in Washington, D.C. See pp48–9

5 Confederate Memorial

Although the cemetery is popularly thought to be only for Union soldiers, 482 Confederate soldiers are buried here as well, in circular rows around a central memorial *(above)*.

7 Tomb of Pierre L'Enfant

Honoring the designer of the city of Washington *(see p36)*, L'Enfant's monument *(below)* shows the plan of the city within a circle.

Plan of Arlington National Cemetery

9 Challenger Shuttle Memorial

This memorial honors the astronauts who died in the explosion of the space shuttle *Challenger* on January 28, 1986, seen live on television across a stunned world.

10 Rough Riders Memorial

This dark granite memorial displays the insignia of the First US Volunteer Cavalry (the "Rough Riders") and the battles they took part in during the Spanish-American War.

Civil War Origins

Robert E Lee was living in Arlington House in 1861 when tensions between the Union and the southern states reached a crisis. When Virginia joined the Confederacy and seceded from the Union, Lee became a general of Virginia's military forces. Union troops then crossed the Potomac and took possession of Arlington House. In 1864, Arlington National Cemetery was established to cope with the mass deaths of the Civil War.

8 Seabees Memorial

A bronze construction worker pauses to make friends with a young child *(below)*. The Seabees – so called from the initials of their name, the Construction Battalion (CB) – performed daring feats in building the military bases needed to win World War II.

6 Grave of John F. Kennedy

The eternal flame *(above)* was lit by Jacqueline Kennedy on the day of the assassinated president's funeral. In 1994 she was buried beside him.

Mount Vernon

This graceful mansion, surrounded by peaceful fields and on the banks of the Potomac River, is second only to the White House as the most visited historic American home. George Washington spent part of his childhood here and returned here after his presidency, taking a great interest in improving the estate. With many of the buildings and activities brought back to life by curators, no other place better portrays the character of the first US president, as well as the role of slavery-based agriculture in the young republic.

Façade

🕐 Visit Mount Vernon after 1pm, when special school programs are over.

The Mount Vernon shops sell seeds of some of the estate's heritage plants.

🍽 Outside the main entrance is a complex with a full-service restaurant, the Mount Vernon Inn, offering specialties such as peanut and chestnut soup and salmon corncakes, and an efficient food court, serving snacks.

• George Washington Parkway
• 703-780-2000
• www.mountvernon. org/index.html
• Open Apr–Aug: 8am–5pm daily; Mar, Sep, Oct: 9am–5pm daily; Nov–Feb: 9am–4pm daily
• Dis. access
• Adm $11.00 adults; $10.50 senior citizens; $5.00 children 6–11 years; free under 6 yrs

Top 10 Features

1. Mansion's Exterior
2. Large Dining Room
3. Front Parlor
4. Little Parlor
5. Study
6. Kitchen
7. Lafayette Bedroom
8. Nellie Custis Room
9. Master Bedroom
10. Cupola

1 Mansion's Exterior

The huge portico that overlooks the Potomac was the president's own design. The house is built from pine, but the exterior was "rusticated" with a decorative treatment that re-creates the look of stone.

2 Large Dining Room

This impressive two-story room *(above)* is formal enough for state business yet is inviting to all. Washington used boards placed on trestles for a table – easier to clear for dancing.

3 Front Parlor

This charming room *(above)* was the main public space in the house. A copy of the earliest known portrait of Washington, by Charles Willson Peale, hangs here.

4 Little Parlor

Many visitors find this room a highlight of the mansion because it reflects the family life lived in the house. The original harpsichord Washington purchased for his step-granddaughter, Nellie Custis, is displayed.

5 Study

This study *(below)* was the setting for Washington's commercial, political, and public work. A famous bust of the president, commissioned by the Virginia Assembly, is displayed. French sculptor Jean Antoine Houdon came to Mount Vernon in 1785 to make a plaster cast of the general's head.

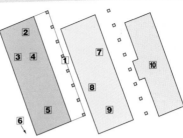

Key

First Floor

Second Floor

Third Floor

9 Master Bedroom

Often called Mrs. Washington's Room *(below)*, this is where George and Martha slept. Mrs. Washington ordered the bed in the 1790s.

6 Kitchen

Mrs Washington directed a staff of slaves in the kitchen *(below)*, and at least two cooks' names have survived, Nathan and Lucy. Much physical labor was required for cooking – fuel and water had to be hauled in by hand.

7 Lafayette Bedroom

This guest bedroom, with its beautiful view of the Potomac, is one of five in the house and is where the Marquis de Lafayette, one of Washington's military aides and a lifelong friend, stayed when visiting.

10 Cupola

The cupola, with its "dove-of-peace" weathervane, provides light to the third floor and aids air circulation in summer.

Building Mount Vernon

The estate that was to be Mount Vernon had been in the Washington family since 1674. George Washington received ownership in 1761 but had already done extensive work on the house and grounds. Additions to the house were underway at the beginning of the Revolutionary War, but the dining room was completed after the war.

8 Nelly Custis Room

Martha Washington's granddaughter, Nelly Custis, lived at Mount Vernon from early childhood. This comfortable room was hers; she even stayed here for a short while after she had married.

Left **16-Sided Treading Barn** Right **Shipping and Receiving Dock**

Features of Mr. Washington's Farm

1 16-Sided Treading Barn

With this unique design, George Washington created one of the most aesthetically pleasing and yet efficient working barns. The circular floorplan of the building with its slatted upper floor allowed horses to tread over grain placed on the floor to break the heads from the stalks. The grain then fell through the slats into temporary storage below. The building seen today is a painstaking reconstruction of the original based on thorough research by numerous archeologists and curators.

2 Shipping and Receiving Dock

The wharf of the plantation was the main transportation center for shipping outbound produce and receiving farming and household supplies. The Potomac River was a major carrier of

Slave Quarters

Upper Garden

passengers and trade goods in Washington's day. At this evocative spot on its banks, it is easy to imagine the bustle and excitement of early commerce on the river.

3 River Tours

Visitors can still use the Potomac River to reach Mount Vernon. Three tour boat lines serve the wharf from the city: Spirit Cruise Line, Old Town Alexandria, and Colonial Farm in Maryland. Spirit Cruise Line also offers lovely summer river sightseeing tours originating and ending at Mount Vernon's wharf. 🕾 *Spirit Cruise Line: 202-554-8000 • Old Town Alexandria: Potomac Riverboat Company: 703-548-9000 • Colonial Farm in Maryland: Accokeek Dory, 301-283-2113*

4 Slave Quarters

Many slaves had living spaces distributed over the plantation so that they were convenient to the work they were assigned. The remaining slaves lived communally in these quarters on the edge of the estate. In his will, Washington freed all his slaves and made provision for their ongoing support. Memorials to his slaves, erected in 1983, are located at the slave burial ground southwest of Washington's tomb, which itself is at the southwest end of the plantation.

5 Upper and Lower Gardens

The wonderfully colorful upper flower garden is densely planted with varieties known to be cultivated in Washington's time. The lower garden is surrounded by boxwood bushes that were planted before Washington's death. This orderly and expansive plot yielded a wealth of vegetables and berries for the plantation. An auditorium in the gardens stages a short but interesting audio-visual presentation about the life of the nation's first president.

6 Crop Experimentation

The extremely handsome greenhouse complex was one place where Washington carried out his extensive experimentation with different plant varieties. He always sought to find potentially profitable new crops for his five farms. Slaves were assigned to tend the wood fires to keep the greenhouse warm in the winter.

7 Livestock

Younger visitors to Mount Vernon love the chance to come face to face with some of the animals typical of colonial farming. Pearl, a Percheron draft horse; Blue, the mule; Penelope, the Ossabaw Island hog; Nellie, the Belgian draft horse; Flopsie, the Hog Island sheep; and Cochise the pinto pony bring alive the animal-oriented culture of 18th-century agriculture.

Pioneer farming methods

8 New Farming Tools

Washington adapted or invented many new farm implements to suit his various agricultural needs. He designed a new shape for a plow, made improvements to a seeding machine with a barrel feeder, and invented a turnip planter.

9 Crop Rotation and Soil Conservation

In Washington's day, agriculture, the backbone of the economy, was being dangerously weakened by the rapid depletion of farming soils. The president was possibly the first farmer to successfully combat this development. He drew up a chart of his fields, and carefully devised planting schedules that would give each field time to be replenished before new crop production began again.

10 Fertilization

There seemed to be no limits to Washington's skills and eagerness for improving farming life. He also pioneered the use of mixing organic matter with natural soil to improve the latter's fertility. He regularly gathered up this material, which included dung, gypsum, and even fish heads, at several sites around the farm.

Left **The British burn Washington, 1814** Right **New Deal workers, 1930s**

TOP 10 Moments in History

1 Foundation of the Federal City

The US Constitution, ratified in 1788, provided for "a District (not exceeding ten Miles square) as may, by Cession of Particular States..., become the Seat of the Government of the United States."

George Washington

2 Layout and Design

In 1790 George Washington selected Pierre Charles L'Enfant, a French engineer, to lay out the city. The plan was influenced by Versailles and the city of Paris.

3 War of 1812

The United States declared war on Britain in 1812, seeking freedom of marine trade and the security of US seamen. In 1814 British troops entered the capital and burned government buildings, including the White House and the Capitol. If it had not rained, the whole city might have burned.

4 Expansion

Thomas Jefferson began western expansion by organizing the Lewis and Clark expedition in 1803. The C&O Canal and the Baltimore and Ohio Railroad provided commerce through the mountains and a period of prosperity. New states were added to the Union, and bitter divisions arose connected to the issue of slavery.

5 Civil War

Conflict between the Union and the seceding southern states began on April 12, 1861, and plunged Washington and the nation into crisis. Union supporters, joined by thousands of blacks escaping slavery in the South, doubled the city's population in four years. Although threatened, the city was never taken by Confederate troops, and when the war ended in 1865, Washington was unharmed.

Civil War victory parade

6 McMillan Plan

The McMillan Plan of 1901, named for its congressional supporter, Senator James McMillan, was the first application of city planning in the US. It created much of the layout of the Mall and President's Park seen today.

For historic homes and buildings in Washington, D.C. **See pp44–5**

7 New Deal
The Roosevelt era (1933–1945) brought tremendous growth to the city. Efforts to bring the nation out of the Great Depression increased the size and number of government agencies, and provided direct funds for construction. Most of the buildings in the Federal Triangle, the completion of the Supreme Court, and the National Gallery of Art were New Deal works.

8 World War II
More than 10 percent of the US population of approximately 115 million was in uniform at the peak of the war, and the central management of these troops remained in Washington.

March on Washington

9 March on Washington
On August 28, 1963, African-American leaders led 250,000 people to rally in front of the Lincoln Memorial in support of equal rights. Dr. Martin Luther King, Jr.'s eloquence in expressing his dream for America, along with the size of the march, gave strong impetus to the struggle for justice for all races.

10 Home Rule
The federal government's policy of maintaining full control over the city was modified with the Home Rule Charter in 1973. This legislation gave the city the power to elect its own mayor, city council, and school board.

Top 10 Citizen Rights of the Constitution

1 Inherent Rights
Freedom of religion, speech, the press, assembly, and seeking redress of citizen grievances.

2 Legality of Arms
The right of the people to keep and bear arms.

3 Quartering of Soldiers
Freedom from housing soldiers in private homes in peacetime and in war, except as prescribed by law.

4 Unjustified Searches
Freedom from unreasonable search and seizure of people, houses, and effects without a warrant.

5 Limits on Prosecutors
A grand jury indictment is required before trial; a person cannot be tried more than once for the same crime; a person cannot be forced to testify against himself; a person's property cannot be confiscated without compensation.

6 Protection of the Accused
Accused persons will be given a trial by a jury of peers, be informed of the charges, be able to confront witnesses, and be represented by counsel.

7 Civil Case Jury Trial
In common law, parties have a right to a trial by jury.

8 Unjust Punishment
The government cannot require excessive bail, impose excessive fines, or use cruel or unusual punishment.

9 Limited Scope
The stated rights do not limit other rights.

10 State Powers
All powers not granted to the US government belong to the states.

Left **James Madison** Right **Funeral of John F. Kennedy**

US Presidents

George Washington

1 George Washington
The United States' first president George Washington (1789–97) was never greater than when he refused to interpret the position of president as equivalent to "king."

2 John Adams
Adams (1797–1801) was among the young nation's most experienced diplomats, having managed affairs in Europe. He was the first US vice president, under Washington.

3 Thomas Jefferson
Jefferson (1801–09) is remembered for his embrace of democracy and his opposition to federal power.

4 James Madison
Madison (1809–17) demurred when he was called "the Father of the Constitution," stating that many minds had contributed, but there is little doubt that the Federalist Papers, which he co-authored, helped gain its ratification.

5 Andrew Jackson
The success of Jackson (1829–37) as a leader in the Battle of New Orleans in 1814–15 made him a national hero. His popularity helped him win battles with Congress and with private business interests over issues such as banking and tariffs.

6 Abraham Lincoln
Unquestionably one of the greatest ever political leaders in any nation, Lincoln (1861–5) overcame inexpressible odds in preserving the Union and beginning the process of freeing slaves.

7 Theodore Roosevelt
The dawning of the 20th century brought an energetic and activist president to the helm. Roosevelt (1901–09) became famous for his military exploits in the Spanish-American war, but is best known for his opposition to business monopolies and pursuing a strong foreign policy. He also established the US national parks system.

Abraham Lincoln

Woodrow Wilson

8 Wilson (1913–21) was a quiet academic who faced the greatest foreign task the nation had seen – participation in World War I. Wilson successfully promoted a legislative program that controlled unfair business practices, reduced tariffs, forbade child labor, and improved the banking system.

Franklin D. Roosevelt

Franklin D. Roosevelt

9 Roosevelt's (1933–45) efforts to overcome the Great Depression never succeeded in the broadest sense, but they inculcated the federal government with a respect for the rights and needs of the common man and the poorest of the poor. He led valiantly during World War II.

John F. Kennedy

10 Kennedy (1961–3) brought an unprecedented style and flair to the presidency and can be credited with possibly the most important action of the 20th century – the prevention of nuclear war over Soviet missiles placed in Cuba. His assassination cut short his pursuit of a plan for progressive social programs, including more freedom and justice for African-Americans.

Top 10 First Ladies

Martha Washington
1 Martha established the role of the First Lady imitated by her successors. She was famous for accompanying George on military campaigns.

Dolley Madison
2 Dolley's social appeal helped her slightly awkward husband tremendously.

Sarah Polk
3 The wife of James K. Polk (1845–9) was a strong force in the administration, writing speeches for the president.

Mary Todd Lincoln
4 Mary's pleasure at being First Lady was marred by the Civil War and her husband's assassination in 1865.

Caroline Harrison
5 The wife of Benjamin Harrison (1889–93) founded the Daughters of the American Revolution *(see p93)*.

Grace Coolidge
6 The wife of Calvin Coolidge (1923–9) had a charm and tact that made her one of America's best-loved women.

Eleanor Roosevelt
7 Eleanor's interests were equal rights and social justice. She greatly increased the diplomatic role of the First Lady.

Jacqueline Kennedy
8 A stylish socialite, Jackie was an instant hit with the public and visiting diplomats.

Hillary Clinton
9 Her early activism created friction with Congress, but her public popularity gave her influence. In 2000 she was elected to the Senate.

Laura Bush
10 A former librarian, the current First Lady has made universal literacy and funding of libraries a national goal.

Left **Corcoran Gallery of Art** Center **Freer Gallery of Art** Right **Hirshhorn Museum**

🔟 Art Galleries

1 National Gallery of Art
Displaying one of the most distinguished art collections in the world, this gallery gives visitors a broad but in-depth look at the development of Western art over the centuries *(see pp20–23)*.

2 Phillips Collection
The Phillips is internationally celebrated for its ravishing collection of Impressionist works, including Renoir's *Luncheon of the Boating Party*, Van Gogh's *Entrance to the Public Gardens in Arles*, and Degas' *Dancers at the Barre*, among others. ◈ *1600 21st St, NW • Map M2 • Open 10am– 5pm Tue–Wed, Fri–Sat, 10am–8:30pm Thu, noon–7pm Sun • Adm • Dis. access*

3 Corcoran Gallery of Art
Corcoran exhibitions tilt toward contemporary media, especially photography. The city's first art museum, and one of the three oldest in the United States, is also housed in one of America's most significant Beaux Arts buildings, designed by Ernest Flagg and completed in 1897 *(see p91)*.

4 Hirshhorn Museum and Sculpture Garden
The Hirshhorn exhibits the most varied modern and contemporary art in Washington, D.C.: its Directions gallery is known for displaying the newest – and sometimes the most controversial – work in the city. The lower level features a selection of items from the permanent collection, while large temporary shows are housed on the second floor, along with modern European sculpture. The third floor displays innovative paintings and sculptures up to the present day *(see p77)*.

5 Renwick Gallery
Many Washingtonians name this gallery as their favorite, not least because it is located in a gorgeous French Renaissance-style building, as well as staging well-organized shows of American crafts. It's also refreshingly quiet in comparison to many other museums and galleries. The second-floor Grand Salon, which has recently been renovated in the style of a 19th-century picture gallery, displays paintings and sculpture and is decorated with period furniture. Permanent and touring exhibitions of fine craftwork fill other parts of the building *(see p91)*.

Renwick Gallery

6 Freer Gallery of Art

The amazing Peacock Room is among the finest and most subtle examples of interior design found anywhere in the city. Created for a London home by James McNeill Whistler, and recreated here, the elegantly painted walls and ceiling served as a complement to a collection of blue-and-white porcelain. A discerning collection of works from Asia fills the spacious display areas. ◈ *Jefferson Drive at 12th St SW • Map P5 • Open 10am–5:30pm daily; Closed Dec 25 • Free • Dis. access*

7 National Museum of African Art

This harmonious building brings architectural features common in Africa to one of the Smithsonian's most innovative museums, built principally underground. The wonderful permanent collection provides the best introduction to the role of art in African culture that one could hope to find *(see p82).*

Uma statue, National Museum of African Art

8 Arthur M. Sackler Gallery

Another of the underground museums of the Smithsonian, the Sackler is a leading center for the study and display of ancient and contemporary Asian art. Its events bring Asian art and philosophies to life, and its occasional presentations of Tibetan monks

carrying out the ritual of sand painting a *mandala* are always huge hits. ◈ *1050 Independence Ave SW • Map Q5 • Open 10am–5:30pm daily; Closed Dec 25 • Free • Dis. access*

9 National Museum of Women in the Arts

This is the only museum in the world dedicated exclusively to displaying the work of women artists, from the Renaissance to the present day. Fascinating and provocative exhibitions explore the work and social role of female artists over the centuries, as well as that of women in general *(see p88).*

10 Kreeger Museum

This relatively unknown museum houses Impressionist works to complement those at the Phillips, painters and sculptors from 1850 to the 1970s, and a collection of traditional works from Africa. ◈ *2401 Foxhall Rd, NW • Map G6 • Open 10am–1pm, 2–5pm Mon–Fri by appt only; 1pm–4pm Sat • Donation • Dis. access (main level and terrace)*

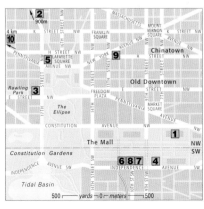

Left **National Air and Space Museum** Right **Dumbarton Oaks**

🔟 Museums

1 National Air and Space Museum

The 20th century's love affair with flight, from its intrepid beginnings to the mastery of space travel, is explored in this wonderful museum *(see pp16–17)*.

2 National Museum of American History

Mixing the "America's Attic" approach with fine contemporary interpretive exhibits, the museum offers a fascinating look at America's past *(see pp18–19)*.

3 National Museum of Natural History

Must-see exhibits abound at this huge museum: the Dinosaur Hall with its 87-ft (27-m) *Diplodocus longus*; skeletal remains; the Hope diamond; the Insect Zoo; and a stunning new O. Orkin IMAX® theater *(see p78)*.

Dinosaur Hall, National Museum of Natural History

4 National Museum of the American Indian

The Smithsonian's huge collection of material and artifacts related to Native American art, history, culture, and language is preparing to move into its first permanent home in Washington in 2004. A temporary Welcome Center has a small exhibit on the plans for the museum and, best of all, a window where you can watch the construction *(see p82)*.

5 United States Holocaust Memorial Museum

An ingeniously symbolic building houses documents depicting the Holocaust in Europe before and during World War II, grimly detailing the surveillance and the loss of individual rights faced by Jews, political objectors, gypsies, homosexuals, and the handicapped. Moving eyewitness accounts, photographs, and artifacts tell the story, from "Nazi Assault," to "Last Chapter" *(see p78)*.

6 National Postal Museum

Mail and fun don't naturally go together, but at this wonderfully conceived museum, they do. The little Pony Express

Personal artifacts, United States Holocaust Memorial Museum

saddlebags, the tunnel-like construction representing the desolate roads faced by the earliest mail carriers, and the mail-sorting railroad car entertain and inform visitors *(see p73)*.

7 Arts and Industries Building

The permanent exhibition here recreates the feel of the Philadelphia Centennial Exposition of 1876. The High Victorian brick and sandstone building opened in 1881 as the original US National Museum, from which sprang the rest of the Smithsonian *(see p82)*.

Bill of Rights, National Archives

8 National Archives

The Rotunda of the National Archives has recently been reorganized, but still proudly displays the foundation documents of American independence and government: the Declaration of Independence, the Constitution of the United States, and the Bill of Rights. The museum also now features exciting interactive activities *(see p82)*.

9 Dumbarton Oaks

The collections of Byzantine and Pre-Columbian art here are among the most important in the world. The elegant Federal-style house was the site of the 1944 meetings that ultimately led to the founding of the United Nations *(see p99)*.

10 Textile Museum

One of the world's foremost specialized museums. Its holdings include over 17,000 objects, spanning 5,000 years, and it maintains one of the finest collections anywhere of Pre-Columbian, Peruvian, Islamic, and Coptic textiles and Oriental carpets. ◈ *2320 S St, NW • Map M1 • Open 10am–5pm Mon–Sat, 1–5pm Sun • Adm*

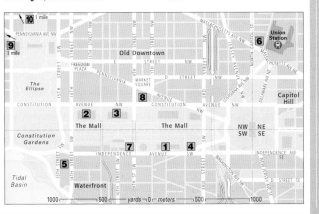

Left **Woodrow Wilson House** Right **Cedar Hill**

Historic Homes and Buildings

1 Ford's Theater
The theater where Lincoln was shot on April 14, 1865 *(see p36)*, has been restored by the federal government and is now a memorial to the president and his love of theater and music *(see p87)*.

2 Decatur House
Stephen Decatur was a renowned naval hero when he built this Federal-style town-house in 1818, but he was killed in a duel 14 months after he moved in. It now evokes the life of 19th-century middle-class America. ◈ *748 Jackson Place NW • Map N3 • Open 10am–3pm Tue–Fri, noon–4pm Sat–Sun • Free*

3 Gadsby's Tavern Museum
George Washington was a patron of this former tavern. The older of the two colonial buildings, dating from 1770, was a

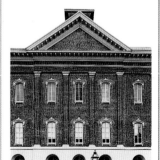

Ford's Theater

going concern six years before the Declaration of Independence. The second building houses a restaurant that serves food typical of the 18th century. ◈ *134 N Royal St, Alexandria, VA • Map D5 • 703-838-4242 • Call for seasonal museum hours • Adm*

4 Carnegie Library
Andrew Carnegie's campaign to build libraries across America (he funded 1,679 in all) changed the country forever. This magnificent Beaux Arts building has been fully restored and is the City Museum operated by the Historical Society of Washington, DC. ◈ *Mt Vernon Sq NW • Map Q3*

5 Woodrow Wilson House
The 28th president was exhausted and demoralized when he left office in 1921, but this Georgian Revival house must have done much to restore his spirits. It now gives a delightful insight into 1920s American life. ◈ *2340 S St NW • Map M1 • Open 10am–4pm Tue–Sun • Adm • Dis. access*

6 Cedar Hill
Frederick Douglass and his wife Anna became the first African-American family in Anacostia when they moved into this estate in 1877. Born a slave, Douglass became America's most effective anti-slavery speaker *(see p46)*. Accessible by Tourmobile *(see p117)*. ◈ *1411 W St SE • Map E4 • Open Apr–Sep: 9am–5pm daily; Oct–Mar: 9am–4pm daily • Dis. access • Adm*

Mary McLeod Bethune Council House

7 Mary McLeod Bethune Council House

The renowned teacher *(see p46)* and advocate for women's and African-Americans' rights bought this Victorian townhouse – now a National Historic Site – in 1935. It is still furnished with her possessions. ✆ *1318 Vermont Ave NW • Map P2 • Open 10am–4pm Mon–Sat • Free*

8 Old Stone House

The oldest surviving structure in DC, this evocative little building holds demonstrations of crafts and skills of pre-Revolutionary life, such as sheep-shearing, and cooking on an open hearth *(see p100)*.

9 Anderson House

This astounding Beaux Arts mansion from 1905 is decorated in the eccentric style of its original resident, Ambassador Larz Anderson. Its 600-ft (180-m) long ballroom is spectacular. ✆ *2118 Massachusetts Ave NW • Map M2 • Open 1–4pm Tue–Sat • Free*

10 Sewell-Belmont House

The 1800 construction date makes this enchanting home one of the oldest on Capitol Hill, and a National Historic Landmark. It is now a museum of women's emancipation *(see p73)*.

Top 10 Architectural Sights

1 National Building Museum

In this cavernous interior, displays examine architecture, engineering, design, and city planning *(see p87)*.

2 Old Executive Office Building

The extravagant decoration is a favorite with architecture buffs *(see p91)*.

3 Treasury Building

This Greek Revival building maintains features from its 1836 beginnings *(see p92)*.

4 The Octagon

This odd-shaped building is now a museum of architecture and design *(see p92)*.

5 Library of Congress

The most extensive library ever built contains exquisite decoration *(see pp24–5)*.

6 Old Post Office Pavilion

A Romanesque revival skyscraper completed in 1899 now contains shops and a food court *(see p57)*.

7 Pope-Leighey House

The city's most innovative Frank Lloyd Wright design. ✆ *Alexandria, VA • US 1 and Rte 235*

8 Supreme Court

This marble edifice never fails to delight *(see p71)*.

9 Gunston Hall

George Mason's refurbished house is luminescent with vivid colors and designs. ✆ *Mason Neck, VA • Rte 242, south of US 1*

10 Cox's Row

Outstanding examples of domestic architecture of the early 19th century. ✆ *3327–39 N St NW • Map K2 • Closed to the public*

Left **Lincoln Memorial** Right **Mary McLeod Bethune Council House**

Places of African-American History

1 Lincoln Memorial
This memorial touches the hearts of all African-Americans because of Lincoln's steadfastness in ending slavery in the US. It was here that Martin Luther King, Jr. made his "I Have a Dream" speech *(see p48)*.

2 Metropolitan African Methodist Episcopal Church
This church was important in sheltering runaway slaves before the Civil War, and its pulpit has hosted many respected speakers, including Frederick Douglass, Martin Luther King, Jr., and Jesse Jackson. ✆ *1518 M St, NW • Map N3*

3 Anacostia Museum and Center for African-American History and Culture
This museum explores the role that African-Americans have played in the culture of the nation. Temporary exhibitions examine specific events or survey the work of important black artists. ✆ *1901 Fort Place, SE • Map E4 • Open 10am–5pm daily • Dis. access • Free*

4 Cedar Hill
Frederick Douglass, a former slave, made many speeches for the rights of African-Americans, and was an adviser to Abraham Lincoln. He and his wife, Anna, moved into this Gothic-Italian-style house in 1877. In the garden is a humble stone hut nicknamed "The Growlery," which Douglass used as a study *(see p44)*.

5 Mary McLeod Bethune Council House
A former cotton-picker, Bethune rose to be a leading educator of African-Americans and an activist for equal rights. Her house was the headquarters of the National Council of Negro Women, which she founded. During the Franklin D. Roosevelt administration, she was a valued adviser *(see p45)*.

6 Supreme Court
In one of its most notable decisions, the Supreme Court aided African-Americans' quest for equality in the 1954 Brown v. Board of Education trial, in which the "separate but equal" system of education was overturned. It was a turnaround from the 1896 Plessy v. Ferguson decision that supported segregation *(see p71)*.

7 Mount Zion United Methodist Church
Believed to be the first black congregation in the District, founded in 1816, Mount Zion's original building was an important stop on the Underground

"The Growlery," Cedar Hill

For more moments in history in Washington, D.C. See pp36–7

Supreme Court

Railroad. Its present red-brick site was built in 1884. Behind the church is a small cottage containing a collection of artifacts reflecting the black history of Georgetown. ◈ 1334 29 St, NW • Map L2 • 202-234-0148 • Open by appt

8 Lincoln Park

This pleasant urban park does justice to its dedication to Abraham Lincoln. The 1974 Robert Berks statue of Mary McLeod Bethune shows the great educator passing the tools of culture on to younger generations. The Emancipation Statue by Thomas Ball (1876) shows Lincoln holding his Proclamation in the presence of a slave escaping his chains (see p74).

9 Frederick Douglass Museum

Another site associated with the statesman and abolitionist, this was Douglass's home for nearly 10 years from the mid-1870s. Artifacts associated with Douglass are displayed here (see p74).

10 Benjamin Banneker Park

This waterfront park is named in honor of a renowned 18th-century free black mathematician and astronomer. ◈ 10th and G Sts, SE • Map Q6

Top 10 African-American Figures

1 Ralph Bunche
The first African-American to receive the Nobel Peace Prize, because of his diplomatic efforts in the UN.

2 Duke Ellington
The musical genius was a native Washingtonian. He played his first paid performance on U Street.

3 Hiram Rhodes Revel
The first African-American to take a seat as US senator, representing Mississippi.

4 Paul Lawrence Dunbar
Dunbar rose from poverty to gain recognition as a poet – the first African-American to do so – publishing his first collection in 1892.

5 Harriet Tubman
The best-known figure who freed slaves through the Underground Railroad.

6 Ida B. Wells-Barnett
This celebrated crusader against anti-black government actions also marched in the 1913 women's suffrage rally.

7 Marian Anderson
In 1939 the singer was barred from Constitution Hall because of her race, so gave her Easter Sunday concert at the Lincoln Memorial instead.

8 Eleanor Holmes Norton
Norton has been effective as the District's non-voting House member, lobbying to promote Washington issues.

9 Walter E. Washington
Mayor of Washington from 1974–8, the first elected mayor in the city for over 100 years.

10 Anthony Williams
Elected mayor in 1998, he has streamlined administrative and fiscal operations.

Left **Jefferson Memorial** Center **Franklin D Roosevelt Memorial** Right **US Navy Memorial**

🔟 Memorials and Monuments

1 Lincoln Memorial

The majestic monument to the president who preserved America's unity and began the long process of ending slavery is built in the form of a Greek temple. Daniel Chester French designed the enormous statue of a seated Abraham Lincoln in 1915, and it is among America's most inspiring sites, especially for its association with African-Americans' struggle for equality and opportunity (see p78).

2 Washington Monument

This spire is the dominant feature on the city skyline, 555 ft (170 m) high and gleaming in its marble cladding. One of the tallest freestanding masonry constructions in the world, built between 1848 and 1884, it offers stunning views from the observation platform (see p78).

3 Jefferson Memorial

One of Jefferson's favorite Classical designs, the Pantheon in Rome, inspired this graceful monument. Dedicated in 1943 on the 200th anniversary of Jefferson's birth, it houses a 19-ft (6-m) bronze statue of the president by Rudolph Evans. It is especially enchanting when floodlit at night (see p82).

4 Franklin Delano Roosevelt Memorial

This popular memorial has four outdoor rooms, representing Roosevelt's four terms as president. Each is a composition of statues, water, plants, and engraved quotations of the president. The memorial has provided a focus for activists for disabled citizens – Roosevelt was partially paralyzed by polio (see p82).

5 Vietnam Veterans' Memorial

This simple structure – a V-shaped black stone wall on which are carved the names of those who died in this divisive war – has moved millions of visitors. The memorial, built in 1982, is the work of Maya Lin, at the time a 21-year-old architecture student at Yale (see p79).

6 Korean War Veterans Memorial

Nineteen exhausted foot soldiers plod forward, determined on their goal. These 7-ft (2-m) steel statues are the dominant element in a memorial to the Americans who died in the UN's "police action" in Korea. A wall is etched with faces of actual soldiers. A circular pool invites quiet reflection (see p82).

Lincoln Memorial

wo Jima Statue (Marine Corps Memorial)

Top 10 Statues

1 Abraham Lincoln
The marble vision dominates Lincoln's memorial.

2 Neptune Fountain
Roland Hinton Perry created this grouping at the Library of Congress *(see p25)*.

3 Albert Einstein
This 1979 bronze by Robert Berks shows the great thinker in front of the National Academy of Sciences. ⓢ *2101 Constitution Ave NW • Map M4*

4 Benjamin Franklin
Jacques Jouvenal's statue at the Old Post Office honors Franklin's creation of the US Postal Service. ⓢ *Pennsylvania Ave & 12th St NW • Map P4*

5 First Division Monument
A shining tribute to the First Infantry Division of World War I ⓢ *State Place & 17th St NW • Map N4*

6 Andrew Jackson
This heroic equestrian statue was created by Clark Mills in 1853. ⓢ *H Street & 16th St NW • Map N3*

7 Winston Churchill
A 1966 sculpture by William M McVey symbolizes the friendship between Britain and the US *(see p54)*.

8 Grant Memorial
This magnificent grouping took Henry Merwin Shrady 20 years to complete *(see p74)*.

9 Theodore Roosevelt
Paul Manship's work shows the president gesticulating to his listeners. ⓢ *Roosevelt Island • Map L4*

10 Joan of Arc
This 1922 work was a gift from the women of France to the women of the US. ⓢ *Meridian Hill Park, Florida Ave & 16th St NW • Map N1*

7 Iwo Jima Statue
Marines struggling to erect the Stars and Stripes on a ridge t Iwo Jima serves as a memorial o all marines who have fought or their country. The small Pacific island was the site of ierce fighting, resulting in nearly ,000 American deaths, during World War II. ⓢ *George Washington arkway (I-66, exit 75), Arlington, VA • Map K5 • Free • Dis. access*

8 World War II Veterans Memorial
his 7.5-acre memorial, being uilt to honor US veterans of World War II, will include commemorative columns, a Freedom Wall, landscaping, and fountains. ⓢ *National Mall • Map P5 • Due to open n 2004 • Free • Dis. access*

9 African-American Civil War Memorial
"The Spirit of Freedom," a 1996 sculpture by Ed Hamilton, depicts African-American Union soldiers acing their enemies. ⓢ *U & 10th ts NW • Map P1 • Free • Dis. access*

10 US Navy Memorial
The fountains that surround nis plaza contain recirculated vater from all the seven seas. lagstaffs suggest the rigging of tall ship *(see p88)*.

Left **Theodore Roosevelt Island** Right **US Botanic Garden**

🔟 Green Spaces

1 US Botanic Garden

The gleaming glass-walled conservatory building is a beautiful home for this "living plant museum." Microclimates, such as desert, oasis, and jungle, reveal the variety and beauty of plant adaptations. Don't miss the primitive ferns and other plants dating back 150 million years. Outside is the variegated National Garden with an environmental learning center (see p72).

2 Enid A. Haupt Garden

This "rooftop" garden is inspired by the culture on display beneath it in the Smithsonian Museums. The Island Garden beside the Sackler Gallery reflects the Asian world, with its moon gate, pools, and cherry and beech trees. The Fountain Garden, next to the Museum of African Art, sets a Moorish tone, with cascading waters and shaded seats.
🌢 10th St & Independence Ave, NW • Map P5 • Open Memorial Day–Sep 30: 6:30am– 8pm daily; Oct–Memorial Day: 7am– 5:45pm daily • Free • Dis. access

3 Dumbarton Oaks

Magnificent trees, including ancient oaks, soar above the park and gardens surrounding this historic Federal-style house. Designed by Beatrix Jones Farrand, the gardens range from formal to more casual settings. From March to October they are ablaze with wisteria, roses, lilies, perennial borders, and chrysanthemums. Pools and fountains tie the verdant ensemble together (see p99).

4 National Arboretum

A world-acclaimed bonsai display – some of the bantam trees are almost 400 years old – forms one of the many collections that flourish season to season on these 446 acres dedicated to research, preservation, and education. Azaleas, dogwoods, holly, magnolias, herbs, roses, and boxwoods abound. A stand of columns, formerly on the US Capitol, adds a classical air. 🌢 3501 New York Ave, NE • Map E3 • Open 8am–5pm daily • Free • Dis. access

US Botanic Garden

5 Rock Creek Park

This vast national park meanders with its namesake creek, offering something for everyone: woodland trails, 30 picnic areas, 25 tennis courts, a golf course, playing fields, and nature programs for kids and adults (see p53).

For outdoor activities in Washington, D.C. See pp60–61

Chinese Pavilion, National Arboretum

6 C&O Canal

Canalboats on this 184-mile (295-km) waterway, dating back to the early 19th century, carried cargo between Maryland and Georgetown for 100 years before the railroad put it out of business. The canal is now a National Historical Park, a haven for walkers and cyclists along its towpath and for canoeists and boaters in its waters. Catch a mule-drawn boat ride at Georgetown or Great Falls *(see p99)*.

7 Theodore Roosevelt Island

This wooded island on the Potomac River is the perfect memorial to the president remembered as a conservationist. A 17-ft (5-m) statue of Teddy Roosevelt is the centerpiece of what otherwise is a monument to nature – a space for birdwatching, hiking, and fishing. ◈ *George Washington Parkway • Map L4 • Open dawn to dusk daily • Free • Dis. access*

8 Bartholdi Park and Fountain

The French sculptor of the Statue of Liberty, Frédéric Auguste Bartholdi (1834–1904), also created this reflection of *belle époque* majesty. The 30-ft (9-m) sculpture's three caryatids support a circular basin surmounted by three tritons. A small garden surrounds the fountain like the setting for a gemstone *(see p72)*.

9 Kenilworth Park and Aquatic Gardens

The 14-acre Aquatic Gardens began as a hobby for W.B. Shaw in 1882, then became a commercial water garden, where Shaw and his daughter developed many varieties of water lilies. Now a national park, the gardens are home to water lilies and lotuses, plus many varieties of birds, frogs, turtles, and butterflies. Adjacent is Kenilworth Park, with acres of recreational areas and tended meadows. ◈ *Gardens: Anacostia Ave, SE; Map E3; Open 8am–4pm daily; Free; Dis. access • Park: Kenilworth & Burroughs aves; Map E3; Open 8am–4pm daily; Free; Dis. access*

10 Glover Archbold Trail

From Van Ness Street to the Potomac River, this 3-mile (5-km) trail in the northwest of the city passes beneath 200-year-old trees that host an abundance of birds, in keeping with its designation as a bird sanctuary in 1924. The trail hooks up with the C&O Canal towpath, and other routes. ◈ *South of Tenleytown Metro station on Wisconsin Ave, then left on Van Ness St, NW*

Pierce Mill, Rock Creek Park

Left **National Air and Space Museum** Right **Capital Children's Museum**

Children's Attractions

1 National Air and Space Museum

Kids' dreams are founded on and inspired by these ravishing soaring devices and spectacular rockets, while their parents and grandparents can reminisce over the early days of aviation and see how far we've come. End the visit by treating children to a scoop of the freeze-dried ice cream *(see pp16–17)*.

2 National Zoological Park

The animals in Washington, D.C.'s zoo are housed in large, recreated natural habitats and are close enough to be clearly observed. Sea lion demonstrations never fail to delight *(see pp28–9)*.

3 National Geographic Society Explorers' Hall

These first-class exhibits explore the major domains of society, including foreign cultures, nature, archaeology, and superb photography. The hall is at the forefront of designing and

National Zoological Park

constructing interactive and immersive displays to involve visitors in their fascinating subject matter. Kids need little direction here – they take to the explorations and activities enthusiastically, sometimes with a more immediate grasp than adults. The well-stocked shop complements the exhibitions. ⊙ *17th & M Sts NW • Map N2 • Open 9am–5pm Mon–Sat, 10am–5pm Sun • Dis. access • Free*

4 MCI Sports Center

Children love the energetic events here. The Ringling Brothers Barnum & Bailey Circus performs here, along with touring ice skating spectaculars, professional wrestling, hockey games and many top-name pop and rock acts. The food is better than usual at an arena and, naturally, is geared toward kids *(see p87)*.

5 Capital Children's Museum

This boisterous, animated site is called a museum, but it's more like a huge indoor playground with superb equipment. Children take to all the subjects immediately, which may include anything from trying their hand at cartoon animation, studying the life of Japanese schoolchildren, exploring firefighting equipment, or making cocoa and tortillas in a recreated Mexican plaza – and best of all, they're learning too *(see p73)*.

6 National Aquarium

Turtle, National Aquarium

The star attraction for children here is the 2pm feedings: sharks on Mondays, Wednesdays, and Saturdays, piranha on Tuesdays, Thursdays, and Sundays, and alligators on Fridays. The aquarium houses about 300 specimens in its glass tanks, and provides easy-to-understand informative material about freshwater habitats and the oceans and the marine life they support. Inquisitive little visitors always surround the touch tank. The staff are extremely friendly and helpful, and children's questions are handled with aplomb *(see p88)*.

7 Discovery Creek Children's Museum

This outdoor-oriented center for children aged between three and eleven years provides wonderfully engrossing activities that bring to life aspects of local nature, arts, and history. Operating from the only one-room schoolhouse surviving in the city, the museum uses the natural setting of beautiful Glen Echo Park for its programs and events. A Friday-morning program for toddlers is always popular with Washingtonians. *5125 MacArthur Blvd, Suite 10 • Map C3 • Open 10am–3pm Sat, 11am–3pm Sun • Adm*

8 Washington Doll's House and Toy Museum

A world of miniatures is set out here, as tantalizing to adults as to children. Tiny shops complete with inventories, a Bauhaus-designed house, several versions of Noah's Ark loaded with its animal passengers, and other unexpected treasures complement the Victorian and early 20th-century dollhouses and toys and fuel the imagination.
Antiques America magazine lists the myriad tiny items in this museum as among the major collections of miniatures in the United States, and it's easy to see why. *5236 44th St NW • Map G2 • Open 10am–5pm Tue–Sat, noon–5pm Sun • Adm*

9 Smithsonian Carousel

In front of the Arts and Industries Building *(see p82)* at the Smithsonian is a delightful authentic carousel with brilliantly painted hand-carved animals. It only operates in good weather, but don't miss this bit of old-world fun if you have the chance. It also makes a refreshing break for kids beginning to tire of the numerous surrounding museums. *900 Jefferson Drive SW • Map P5 • Open 10am–5pm daily • Adm*

10 Rock Creek Park Nature Center

The short nature trail here is only 1-mile (1.5-km) long *(see p51)* so it is easily negotiated by children. Many native species can be spotted en route, including foxes, racoons and deer. There is also a small planetarium. A number of activities that appeal to children, including arts and crafts workshops, are scheduled throughout the year. On a sunny day, this is also a great place to bring a picnic, and enjoy one of the city's truly natural environments. In other parts of the park there are also tennis courts and horse riding trails. *5200 Glover Rd NW • Map J2 • Open 9am–5pm Wed–Sun • Free*

Left **Washington Post newsroom during the Watergate scandal** Right **Dumbarton Oaks**

Places of Politics and Intrigue

1 Embassy Row

Since the 19th century, Embassy Row, the string of great mansions heading west from Dupont Circle up Massachusetts Avenue, has been a hotbed of gathering and suppressing information. Today, 46 embassies and chanceries here help shape foreign policy by allowing issues to be discussed without the glare of public announcement. ◈ *Map N2*

Churchill statue, Embassy Row

2 Watergate and Washington Post Newsroom

The Watergate complex became the most infamous apartment and office complex in the world when a bungled burglary there, as part of an espionage campaign against President Nixon's opponents, led to his resignation *(see p96)*. The newspaper that played the main role in revealing the scandal, the *Washington Post*, offers tours to groups on Mondays (write to request a tour two weeks in advance). ◈ *Watergate: Virginia Ave, NW; Map M3 • Washington Post newsroom: 1150 15th St, NW • Map P3 • 202-334-7969*

Watergate complex

3 Katherine Graham House

The Georgetown home of Katherine Graham, publisher of the *Washington Post* from 1963 to 2001, provided a salon for politicians of every persuasion to discuss issues of the day. ◈ *2920 R St NW • Map L2 • Closed to the public*

4 Dumbarton Oaks

In 1944, representatives of China, the Soviet Union, United Kingdom, and the United States developed proposals at Dumbarton Oaks for an international body to bring peace among nations. The result was the United Nations *(see p99)*

5 International Spy Museum

This fascinating museum examines clandestine operations in political and military decisions. Artifacts include an example of Enigma, the World War II German encryption device, and a camera designed to photograph through walls. ◈ *800 F St, NW • Map Q4 • Open Apr–Oct: 10am–8pm daily; Nov–Mar: 10am–6pm daily • Dis. access • Adm*

6 Private Clubs

Lobbyists regularly frequent private clubs in the downtown area, such as the National Democratic Club and Army and Navy Club, as well as country clubs such as the Congressional Country Club, where a little discreet politicking is accepted and expected.

For political scandals in Washington, D.C. **See p96**

House of the Temple Library

7

This is a serious library with many rare items, but many people find its appeal in the insights it offers into famous Washingtonians, especially the large display on J. Edgar Hoover. ⊗ *1733 16th St, NW • Map N2 • Open 8am–3:45pm Mon–Fri • 202-232-3579*

House of the Temple Library

FedEx Field

8

The Washington Redskins are something of a local religion *(see p61)*. At home games, the cigar bar, club seating levels, and luxurious suite- and box-seating are filled with lobbyists, campaign donors, and activists schmoozing with each other.

Political Dining

9

The Monocle has a history of fostering alliances and deals – it is the closest restaurant to the Senate side of the Capitol. The Caucus Room *(see p63)* is largely funded by political insiders, and popular for high-profile power-dining. ⊗ *The Monocle: 107 D St, NE • Map S4 • 202-546-4488 • $$$*

The Inn at Little Washington

10

This famed restaurant, west of the city, is a prime spot for entertaining to impress, and the one-hour drive there and back provides time for lobbyists to bond and bargain – assuming the car is bug-free. ⊗ *Middle & Main sts, Washington, VA • 540-675-3800 • $$$$$*

Top 10 Congressional Leaders in History

1 **James K. Polk**
A supporter of Andrew Jackson, Polk (1795–1849) led the fight in the administration's conflict with the banks. He became president in 1845.

2 **Daniel Webster**
Webster (1782–1852) is credited as the finest speaker in defense of the Union in debates over slavery.

3 **Henry Clay**
A great orator (1777–1852) known for his proposals for compromise over slavery.

4 **William Boyd Allison**
Allison (1829–1908) was a major force in shaping US laws passed in the 19th century.

5 **Henry Cabot Lodge**
This distinguished patrician (1850–1924) opposed corrupt influences of big business.

6 **George W. Norris**
Norris (1861–1944) was author of the 20th Amendment to the US Constitution, clarifying issues related to tenure in office.

7 **Joseph Taylor Robinson**
The death of this leader (1872–1937) was attributed to overwork associated with New Deal proposals *(see p37)*.

8 **Margaret Chase Smith**
Smith (1897–1995) publicly condemned the anti-Communist smear tactics of Senator Joseph McCarthy.

9 **Sam T. Rayburn**
Rayburn (1882–1961) witnessed the administrations of eight presidents.

10 **John W. McCormack**
McCormack (1891–1980) was instrumental in passing the Civil Rights Acts of 1964 and 1968.

Washington, D.C.'s Top 10

Left **Neiman Marcus, Friendship Heights** Right **Georgetown shops**

🔟 Shopping Areas

1 The Fashion Centre at Pentagon City

The local cliché is that this expansive mall has become the new downtown shopping area, even though it is not in the city center. But it is less than 10 minutes away by metro, and there is a train stop right in the mall. Nordstrom and Macy's are the anchors here, but there are over 170 other establishments, including Abercrombie & Fitch, Banana Republic, and Joseph A. Banks. A food court, cinema, and restaurants complete the attractions. ✪ *1100 S Hayes St • Dis. access*

2 Shops at Georgetown Park

This wonderfully restored building – a former stable, power generation plant, and repair shop for streetcars – is worth seeing in itself. It is extraordinarily airy and quiet for a mall. There are high-quality fashions, art, home furnishings, jewelry, and kitchenware. The food court is small but pleasant. ✪ *3222 M St, NW • Map L3 • Dis. access*

3 Friendship Heights

This area in the far north-west of the city is home to some of the most elegant and exclusive retail outlets in the city. Mazza Gallerie is a small, upscale mall at 5300 Wisconsin Ave, NW. Kron Chocolatier *(see p112)* is here, along with Neiman Marcus, Saks Fifth Avenue Men's Store, and Williams-Sonoma

Grande Cuisine. Other stores on Wisconsin Avenue include Tiffany & Co (No. 5500), St- Laurent Rive Gauche (No. 5516), and Cartier (No.5454). ✪ *Map G2*

4 Potomac Mills Mall

This is among the best-known discount outlet malls on the East Coast and one of the largest in the world. Over 220 stores have discounts up to 70 percent off suggested retail prices. Their own in-mall TV station broadcasts special deals and newly available products. A shuttle bus runs from a number of stops in the metropolitan area. ✪ *2700 Potomac Mills Circle 307, Woodbridge, VA • Dis. access*

5 The Shops at National Place

This mall is worth a visit even for nonshoppers. The architecture in the four-story space is inspired, and there are quiet areas to have a coffee. The 40 shops are mainly boutiques and small emporiums. ✪ *529 14th St or 1331 Pennsylvania Ave, NW • Map P4 • Dis. access*

National Place

For tips on shopping in Washington, D.C. See p120

Old Post Office Pavilion

6 Tysons Corner Center and Galleria at Tysons II

This huge shopping complex has many anchor stores – Nordstrom, Bloomingdale's, JC Penney, Hecht's, Lord & Taylor, Saks Fifth Avenue, Macy's, and Neiman Marcus. Two separate malls are separated by Chain Bridge Road. There's plenty of parking, and some hotels run shuttle buses. *Tysons Corner Center: 1961 Chain Bridge Rd, McLean, VA • Galleria at Tysons II: 2001 International Drive, McLean, VA; Dis. access*

7 Watergate Mall

This small shopping area includes St-Laurent Rive Gauche, Valentino, and Saks Jandel. The wares are expensive, but fashion seekers sometimes find sales bargains. ⊗ *2650 Virginia Ave, NW • Map M3 • Dis. access*

8 Georgetown

Probably the most famous shopping area in the city, partly because of the hundreds of shops but also for the pervasive sense of style. Fashion shops are especially numerous, but antiques, art, books, records, electronics, wine, and other products are found here. The main area is between K and T and 27th and 38th streets, NW, especially on Wisconsin Avenue, NW, and M Street, NW. ⊗ *Map L2*

9 Old Post Office Pavilion

This small downtown indoor mall has a number of boutiques and specialty stores selling gifts, collectibles, leather items, video products, and stationery and cards. Ticketplace, with discount tickets for many same-day performances *(see p122)*, is here. The food court on the lower level is extremely popular. ⊗ *12th St & Pennsylvania Ave, NW • Map P4 • Dis. access*

10 Eastern Market

The market is an appetizing source of picnic provisions any day of the week and a swarming carnival of all kinds of arts and crafts vendors on weekends. The big Eastern Market Flea Market is across 7th Street, SE, on Saturdays. Several shops – notably a vintage clothing store and an antiques dealer – and cafés are also located on the same block. On the Eastern Market side of the street (west side) between the market and Pennsylvania Avenue, SE are several shops selling toys and children's items, books, art and prints, imported goods from Asia and South America *(see p74)*.

Eastern Market

Left **National Theatre** Right **Warner Theater**

Theaters

1 Ford's Theater
The tragedy of Lincoln's assassination here in 1865 kept this theater closed for over 100 years, but now it is the home of a vibrant theater company as well as being a museum and historic landmark. Top-notch performers and directors stage plays expressing human values in a multicultural world *(see p87)*.

2 Arena Stage
Internationally renowned as a pioneering theater, for over five decades Arena has produced some of the highest quality drama anywhere. Its three theater spaces present as many as 24 performances each week of innovative, award-winning plays. ◈ *1101 6th St SW • Map Q6*

Auditorium, Ford's Theater

3 Shakespeare Theatre
Top actors, directors, designers, and lighting experts are involved in every dazzling production here. Although specializing in Shakespeare, the company also mounts works by other playwrights *(see p71)*. ◈ *450 7th St NW • Map Q4*

4 National Theatre
A wonderful venue for touring shows, the National Theatre opened in 1835. Since then every US president has attended at least one of its performances. Many Broadway hits have staged their premiere here, including *Showboat* and *West Side Story*. ◈ *1321 Pennsylvania Ave NW • Map P4*

5 Kennedy Center
From Shakespeare to Sondheim, from gripping drama to light-hearted comedies and musicals, the many theater productions at this landmark arts center are almost always critically acclaimed. There are a variety of performance spaces catering to different styles, seating from just a few hundred people to more than 2,000 *(see p91)*.

6 Source Theater Company
The challenging productions of this nonprofit company allow authors, directors, and actors to deeply explore characters and their social and political situations. ◈ *1835 14th St NW • Map P1 • Dis. access*

Shakespeare Theatre

7 Folger Theater
Visitors get a unique experience in the Elizabethan Theatre, which strongly suggests the setting in which Shakespeare's works were originally performed. Works of the Bard and his near contemporaries are featured, and performances of medieval and baroque music fill the schedule *(see p71)*.

8 Gala Hispanic Theater
The recipient of a huge number of awards, this theater mounts works in Spanish with simultaneous English translation. Brilliant productions of works from the classical to the absurd attract a diverse audience. ❧ *1021 7th St NW • Map Q3*

9 Studio Theater
Off-Broadway hits, classics, and experimental fare make up the season at this performance landmark. Two theater spaces are available for the engrossing and often splendid productions here. ❧ *1333 P St NW • Map P2*

10 Church Street Theater
This extraordinarily inviting small theater is used by a number of local companies for productions of all types. With high ceilings and about 100 seats, it is renowned as a venue for interesting work. ❧ *1742 Church St NW • Map N2*

Top 10 Entertainment Venues

1 MCI Center
The home of D.C.'s basketball and hockey teams has many attractions beyond the games *(see p87)*.

2 Warner Theater
You'll find Broadway shows, comedians, and rock concerts here. ❧ *13th & E Sts NW • Map P4*

3 Carter Barron Amphitheater
Best known for the Shakespeare Free For All *(see p64)*. ❧ *4850 Colorado Ave NW • Map D2*

4 Coolidge Auditorium
The home of the library's music series *(see p25)*. ❧ *Library of Congress, 10 1st St SE • Map S5*

5 Lisner Auditorium
This university theater features everything from world music to orchestras. ❧ *21st and H sts NW • Map M3*

6 RFK Stadium
Home to two soccer teams as well as rock festivals. ❧ *2400 E Capitol St SE • Map E4*

7 DAR Constitution Hall
The largest concert hall in D.C. ❧ *1776 D St NW • Map N4 • Dis. access*

8 Lincoln Theater
An intimate setting for jazz, soul, and gospel music. ❧ *1215 U St NW • Map P1*

9 Wolf Trap
An open-air venue for big names in entertainment. ❧ *1551 Trap Rd, Vienna, VA • Metro West Falls Church*

10 Nissan Pavilion
Rock stars perform at this open-air arena. ❧ *7800 Cellar Door Drive, Bristow, VA • Rte I-66 to exit 44*

Washington, D.C.'s Top 10

Left **In-line skaters** Right **Kayaking**

Outdoor Activities

1 Boating

Thompson Boat Center in Georgetown rents kayaks and canoes to reach Roosevelt Island and tour the waterfront. The Washington Sailing Marina rents sailboats for excursions on the Potomac. Call about certification requirements. ◎ *Thompson Boat Center: 2900 Virginia Ave, NW; 202-333-9543; Open Apr–Oct: 6am–8pm daily • Washington Sailing Marina: 1 Marina Drive, Alexandria, VA; 703-548-9027; Open Apr–Oct: 9am–6pm daily*

2 In-Line Skating

In-line skating on the streets is common in the downtown area. Rock Creek Park has been named one of the top 10 sites in the nation for in-line skating, but most bike trails allow skaters as well. The Ski Center rents skates and protective gear. ◎ *Ski Center, 4300 Fordham Rd, NW • Map C3*

3 Running

Runners are everywhere in Washington. The Mall is popular, as are the walkways around the Tidal Basin, Georgetown Waterfront, the C&O Canal *(see p99)*, and Rock Creek Park *(see p50)*.

Runners

Cyclists

4 Cycling

Both Thompson Boat Center and the Washington Sailing Marina rent bicycles. The C&O Canal towpath is easy to reach and very scenic. Another favorite route is the Mount Vernon Trail along the George Washington Parkway to Mount Vernon *(see pp32–5)*. City Bikes can give advice on where to ride. ◎ *City Bikes: 2501 Champlain St, NW, Adams Morgan • Map N1*

5 Golf

There are over 100 golf courses in the vicinity. The famed Congressional Country Club private course in Bethesda is one of the most historic in the world. The East Potomac Park course is public, as is the Rock Creek Park Golf Course. Langston Golf Course was among the first African-American courses in the country. ◎ *East Potomac Park: 972 Ohio Drive, SW; Map D4 • Rock Creek Park Golf Course: 16th St & Rittenhouse Rd, NW; Map D2 • Langston Golf Course: 26th St at Benning Rd, NE; Map D2*

Amateur soccer game

6 Hiking
The 4-mile (7-km) Western Ridge Trail and the 5-mile (8-km) Valley Trail, both in Rock Creek Park (see p50), are scenic and gentle. The 11.5-mile (18.5-km) Capital Crescent Trail follows the old B&O Railroad route through Georgetown north to Bethesda. Trail information is available at www.washdc.org/trail.html.

7 Informal Team Sports
Volleyball, dodge ball, rugby, softball, team Frisbee, and even polo are played on various fields at the western end of the Mall.

8 Tennis
The East Potomac Park Tennis Center is operated by the National Park Service. Indoor and outdoor courts are available. Ⓢ East Potomac Park Tennis Center: Ohio Drive, SW • Map D4

9 Horseback Riding
The Rock Creek Park Horse Center provides scheduled trail rides and riding lessons for all levels. No experience is necessary for the guided rides, and the center provides the required helmet and other necessary equipment. Ⓢ Rock Creek Horse Center: 5100 Glover Rd, NW • Map C2

10 Climbing
The city of Rockville has a climbing gym in its Civic Center Park. Ⓢ 301-309-3182, www.ci. rockville.md.us/recreation/climbing

Top 10 Spectator Sports

1 Washington Redskins
The National Football League Redskins are a year-round obsession. Games are at FedEx Field in Maryland. No single-game tickets are sold.

2 Washington Wizards
The National Basketball Association team plays at the MCI Center (see p87). Tickets are available at the box office.

3 Washington Capitals
The National Hockey League team plays home games at the MCI Center.

4 DC United
Robert F. Kennedy Stadium is home to professional soccer games. Ⓢ Robert F. Kennedy Stadium: 2400 E Capitol St, SE • 202-547-9077

5 Baltimore Orioles
American League baseball at Camden Yards in Baltimore.

6 Washington Mystics
The women's basketball professional league plays home games at the MCI Center.

7 Washington Freedom
Professional women's soccer draws young fans to the RFK Stadium.

8 Georgetown University Basketball
Fast-paced action at the MCI Center.

9 University of Maryland Athletics
ACC champion football and national champion basketball teams lead this varied sports program. Ⓢ College Park, MD • 202-432-SEAT

10 Naval Academy Football
The spectacle and tradition at these games is unmatched. Schedule and ticket information at 800-USA-NAVY.

Left **Madam's Organ** Center **The Improv** Right **Birchmere** right

🔟 Nightspots

1 Blues Alley
Marvelous drinks, food, and snacks in an intimate club setting featuring today's best jazz and cabaret performers *(see p105)*.

2 Madam's Organ
For years this Adams Morgan fixture has defined the middle-of-the-road club scene in the city. Live music and dancing. Their slogan is "Where the Beautiful People go to get ugly." ◈ *2461 18th St, NW • Map N1*

3 Chi-Cha Lounge
A touch of the exotic – such as a hookah with apple-juice-soaked tobacco – but mainly a comfortable bar with live jazz, and exceptional snacks. Chi-cha is a kind of Latin American beverage. ◈ *1624 U St, NW • Map N1*

4 9:30 Club
Edgy, creative live music by some of the best national bands and performers, in a straight stand-up-and-play atmosphere. The young crowds are boisterous and know their music. ◈ *815 V St, NW • Map N1*

5 The Improv
The local establishment of the chain of comedy clubs books some outstanding talents. The restaurant serves a full menu. ◈ *1140 Connecticut Ave, NW • Map N3*

6 Birchmere
Billing itself as a "music hall," the Birchmere has continually presented the very top folk, country, blues, bluegrass, and, recently, swing bands. Good snacks and a full bar. ◈ *3701 Mt Vernon Ave, Alexandria, VA • Map C6*

7 Brickskeller Saloon-Bar
A relaxed bar with hundreds of brands of beer. They sponsor tastings and events. ◈ *1523 22nd St, NW • Map M2*

8 Zanzibar on the Waterfront
This large club overlooking Washington Channel is *the* place to be for African-Americans and Latinos. It's far from segregated: if you can dance, you're welcome. ◈ *700 Water St, SW • Map Q6*

9 Habana Village
The dance hall is packed with patrons working out to salsa, merengue, and tango music. ◈ *1834 Columbia Rd, NW • Map N1*

10 Nation
This vast warehouse draws crowds of serious partygoers. There is a rave on Friday nights, and a high-energy gay dance on Saturday. ◈ *1015 Half St, SE • Map P5*

Blues Alley

Left **Citronelle** Center **Kinkead's** Right **Nora**

🔟 Restaurants

1 Citronelle
Condé Nast *Traveler* magazine named this one of the 50 most exciting restaurants in the world. Both the cuisine and the decor are inventive *(see p105)*.

2 Kinkead's
A power-dining venue, best known for its fine seafood dishes *(see p97)*.

3 Nora
Refined New American cuisine made from organically grown ingredients – including the coffee and chocolate. ⬤ *2132 Florida Ave, NW • Map R2 • $$$*

4 Galileo
Classic northern Italian cooking. The menu is determined by in-season ingredients *(see p97)*.

5 Obelisk
A fixed-price menu of the finest Italian dishes using fresh, in-season ingredients *(see p97)*.

6 Willard Room
In this gorgeous dining environment, the well-trained staff serve French-inspired dishes *(see p89)*.

7 The Caucus Room
Where legislators meet to hammer out agreements. Classic steak and seafood. ⬤ *401 9th St, NW • Map Q4 • $$$*

8 Jaleo
Ravishing flavors burst from a generous selection of *tapas* at this popular restaurant *(see p89)*.

9 Melrose
This hotel restaurant provides a relaxed atmosphere. Live jazz Saturday night. ⬤ *Park Hyatt Washington, 1201 24th St, NW • 202-419-6755 • Map M3 • $$$*

10 1789
Federal-style townhouse serving a medley of lamb, oysters, and other dishes *(see p105)*.

Left **Smithsonian Folklife Festival** Right **National Cherry Blossom Festival**

Festivals and Cultural Events

1 Smithsonian Folklife Festival

Fascinating and entertaining cooking, storytelling, craft-making, dancing, music, and art fill the National Mall for two weeks around Independence Day (July 4). One of the largest and best cultural events in the world.

2 National Cherry Blossom Festival

The Tidal Basin is surrounded by beautiful Japanese cherry trees, which originated with 3,000 specimens given to the city in 1912 by the mayor of Tokyo. The festival celebrating their spring bloom includes a parade, performances, and such offbeat events as a sushi-making contest. ◈ Late Mar–early April

3 Shakespeare Free for All

The first two weeks of June bring free performances of works of Shakespeare in the outdoor theater in Rock Creek Park. Presented by the Shakespeare Theater (see p58), the productions are of excellent quality. Free tickets available at several sites.

Smithsonian Folklife Festival

4 Washington Flower and Garden Show

At the end of winter, locals and visitors alike are revitalized by the early jolt of spring provided by the riot of colorful flowers and inviting landscapes recreated indoors. The air itself is restorative, scented by blossoms. ◈ Washington Convention Center, 900 9th St, NW • Map Q3 • Early Mar

5 Taste of D.C.

This three-day event in mid-October fills a seven-block section of Pennsylvania Avenue (between 7th and 14th Sts) with vendors preparing and selling most of the myriad types of cuisine available in this very international city. Hundreds of other activities pulse at dozens of venues – music, dance, poetry, children's games, comedy acts, and crafts demonstrations and sales. Over a million people attend this exciting food festival.

6 Washington National Cathedral Christmas Services

In early December, the cathedral (see pp26–7) inaugurates the Christmas season with an open house featuring bagpipes, group singing, pageantry, and stunning seasonal decorations. Then, throughout the season, music and concerts are presented, culminating with the elaborate celebrations of Christmas Eve and Christmas Day.

Washington Flower and Garden Show

7 Filmfest D.C.

This top-quality and lively film festival has brought the best of world cinema to the city for over 15 years. The most exciting new films are shown during two weeks in April at various venues, and discussions and film-oriented events are held at theaters, auditoriums, and cafés.

8 Wolf Trap Jazz and Blues Festival

This three-day festival presents some of the best performers of both traditional and contemporary jazz and blues. The all-day Saturday show is an energetic blast. ⬡ Wolf Trap Filene Center, 1551 Trap Rd, Vienna, VA • 703-218-6500 • Jun

9 National Grand Prix

More than just an auto race, this three-day stop on the American Le Mans Series includes enough performances and concerts, celebrity events, exhibitions, and food to qualify as a festival. ⬡ RFK Stadium, 24th and E Capitol Sts, SE • Map E4 • 202-432-SEAT • Mid-Jul

10 Chinese New Year

Ten days of parades, fireworks, special menus at the restaurants, and unique events in Chinatown. Simply pass through the ornate arch at 7th and H streets, NW. ⬡ Late Jan–early Feb

Top 10 One-Day Events

1 Smithsonian Kite Festival
Competitions include home-built kites, fighting kites, and others. ⬡ National Mall • Late Mar–early Apr

2 Independence Day
The celebration culminates with a fireworks display synchronized with patriotic music. ⬡ National Mall • Jul 4

3 White House Easter Egg Roll
White House staff dye eggs for children to seek out on the lawn. ⬡ Easter Mon

4 National Christmas Tree Lighting
The decorations are joyous. ⬡ The Ellipse • Early Dec

5 National Frisbee Festival
The Frisbee dogs always steal the show. ⬡ Washington Monument • Late Aug

6 Mary McLeod Bethune Annual Celebration
Gospel choirs celebrate the African-American educator. ⬡ Lincoln Park • Early Jul

7 National Symphony Labor Day Concert
The official end of summer. ⬡ US Capitol • Labor Day

8 International Gold Cup Steeplechase Races
Take place at the peak of fall's colored foliage. ⬡ Great Meadows Events Centers, The Plains, VA • Mid-Oct

9 St Patrick's Day
A parade on Constitution Ave, SE. ⬡ Sun before Mar 17

10 Martin Luther King, Jr. Day
Church services held. Check local papers for details. ⬡ 3rd Mon in Jan

For current information about the annual Filmfest, visit their website at www.filmfestdc.org

Left **John Brown's fort, Harper's Ferry** Center **Whiteoak Canyon, Skyline Drive** Right **Baltimore**

🔟 Excursions from Washington

1 Annapolis, Maryland

This enticing city on the Chesapeake Bay is one of the great sailing centers on the East Coast as well as being home to the US Naval Academy. It has a bustling business district and numerous historic houses, such as the home of William Paca, the governor who signed the Declaration of Independence. ⊗ *Rte 50 • William Paca House: 186 Prince George St; Open Mar–Dec: 10am–5pm Mon–Sat, noon–5pm Sun*

2 Harpers Ferry, West Virginia

Before the Civil War, John Brown carried out his famous raid against government troops here, protesting the legality of slavery in the United States. The picturesque little town around the old Potomac waterfront has been preserved and is filled with exhibits about the history of this important industrial, shipping, and military center. This is a fine place to hike, and picnics on the riverfront are popular. ⊗ *Rte 340*

3 Skyline Drive, Virginia

This delightful winding road passes 107 miles (170 km) through the mountain and valley scenery of Virginia's Shenandoah National Park. Numerous hiking trails to isolated peaks, waterfalls, and rare forest environments begin from the main highway. ⊗ *Off Rte I-66*

4 Baltimore, Maryland

Called "Charm City" by its residents and promoters, Baltimore offers museums of art, industry, baseball, science, railroads, and marine trade along with historic sites from every American period. Its phenomenal National Aquarium is among the finest in the world. The historic Lexington Market, established in 1782, is still going strong with over 140 food vendors. ⊗ *Rte I-95*

5 Chincoteague and Assateague, Virginia

Assateague Island is famed for its wild ponies. The pony swim and auction, held on the last Wednesday and Thursday of July, is a major attraction. The Chincoteague National Wildlife Refuge is paradise for bird-watchers and nature buffs. The local seafood is first-rate, and the ice cream made here is justifiably famous. ⊗ *Off Rte 13*

William Paca House, Annapolis

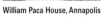

6 Middleburg

In the heart of Virginia hunt country, Middleburg is a captivating little town. Its seasonal farmers market, local horse races, and its antique shops, galleries, and fine restaurants draw visitors from all over.
⊗ Rte 50
• Farmers Market: mid-May–mid-Nov: Sat

The Red Fox Inn, Middleburg

7 Fredericksburg, Virginia

This city on the Rappahannock River offers colonial homes, moving Civil War sites, and a downtown filled with shops and restaurants. A marked walking tour lays out milestones in the city's history. ⊗ Rte 1

8 Frederick, Maryland

Noted for its bridges, Frederick is a city steeped in the memory of 19th-century life and the Civil War. In addition, it has an exceptional artistic and cultural life. ⊗ Rte I-270

9 Manassas Battlefield

This Civil War battlefield is where Confederate and Union soldiers fell by the thousands fighting for conflicting visions of the nation's future. Manassas experienced two pitched battles, the first an opening confrontation of untested troops, the second a bloodbath. Guided tours are available. ⊗ Off Rte I-66

10 Gettysburg, Pennsylvania

The three-day battle of Gettysburg in 1863 was the bloodiest of the Civil War, killing over 51,000. Lincoln's famous address dedicating the cemetery here expressed determination to persevere in maintaining the Union and began to put the great conflict in perspective. The Gettysburg National Military Park is among the most visited sites on the East Coast. ⊗ Rte 15

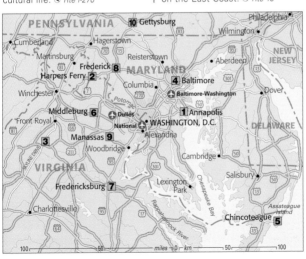

AROUND TOWN

WASHINGTON, D.C'S TOP 10

Left **Library of Congress** Right **Supreme Court Building**

Around Capitol Hill

BUSTLING WITH THE BUSINESS OF GOVERNMENT, *Capitol Hill is also a destination for shopping, entertainment, food and drink, or simply strolling its handsome neighborhood streets. Approached from the west, the area begins with the meticulously landscaped US Capitol complex, which, in addition to the Capitol itself and its giant staff office buildings, includes the splendidly renovated US Botanic Garden, the stately Supreme Court Building, and the three buildings of the Library of Congress. Union Station, to the north, is filled with diverse shops and restaurants and is one of the finest railroad terminals in the world. Farther to the east, beyond the Capitol, lies the residential area, containing streetfuls of pleasing East Coast domestic architecture. Eastern Market on 7th St, SE, serves as a community center, and a pleasant walk farther to the east leads to Lincoln Park, with its outstanding memorial statues (see p74), beginning at 11th St.*

Statue, Sewall-Belmont House

10 Sights

1. US Capitol
2. Library of Congress
3. Union Station
4. Folger Shakespeare Library and Theater
5. Supreme Court Building
6. US Botanic Garden
7. Bartholdi Park and Fountain
8. Sewall-Belmont House
9. Capital Children's Museum
10. National Postal Museum

1 US Capitol
Symbolizing both government power and the control of that power by the people, the Capitol crowns the east end of the National Mall *(see pp10–11)*.

2 Library of Congress
The world's largest collection of books, documents, and sound and video recordings is housed in three huge buildings to the east of the Capitol. The architecture of the Jefferson Building makes it a tourist destination in itself *(see pp24–5)*.

3 Union Station
Opened in 1907, this magnificent Beaux Arts building is still a fully functional transportation hub. The lofty barrel-vaulted concourse, decorated with 70 lbs (32 kg) of gleaming gold leaf, is one of the great public spaces in the city – the Washington Monument, laid on its side, would easily fit within its length. Over 23 million people pass through the station each year. A $160 million restoration, completed in 1988, made the terminal an important retail and entertainment center, with over 130 shops, numerous restaurants, and a 9-screen cinema, as well as expanding its transportation role. ⚓ *50 Massachusetts Ave, NE • Map R4 • Dis. access*

Folger Shakespeare Library and Theater

4 Folger Shakespeare Library and Theater
The Folger has the world's largest library of printed editions of Shakespeare's works, and fascinating displays give viewers an insight into Shakespeare and his times. There is also a huge supporting collection of Renaissance works in other fields, as well as playbills, musical instruments, and costumes. The elegant Neo-Classical building, a 1929 design by Paul Philippe Cret, is on the National Register of Historic Places *(see p58)*. ⚓ *201 East Capitol St, SE • Map S5 • Open 10am– 4pm Mon–Sat • Dis. access • Free*

5 Supreme Court Building
The home of the highest seat of the judicial branch of the US government is a solid and handsome Neo-Classical building designed by Cass Gilbert – the architect of the beautiful Woolworth Building in New York City – and completed in 1935. On its west pediment, above the marble columns of the main entrance, is inscribed in bold letters the famous motto "Equal Justice Under Law" *(see p46)*. ⚓ *1st St and East Capitol St, NE • Map S4 • Open Mon–Fri 9am–4:30pm except federal holidays • Dis. access • Free*

Union Station

Capitol Hill Residences

In the early 19th century, the area east of the Capitol was filled with a motley collection of boarding houses and taverns where members of Congress stayed during legislative sessions. During the 19th and into the 20th centuries, a diverse mix of housing styles – Federal townhouses, manor houses, Queen Anne, interspersed with two-story frame dwellings – developed. The protected Capitol Hill Historic District is now the largest historic residential district in the city.

6 US Botanic Garden

Long valued by Capitol Hill residents as a quiet retreat, the Botanic Garden conservatory is better than ever after its recent four-year restoration. The 4,000 living plants here are arranged into themes and biosystems, such as Plant Exploration, Jungle, Oasis, Medicinal Plants, and many others. The wedge-shaped National Garden, adjacent to the west, includes glorious outdoor displays in a water garden, a rose garden, and a showcase garden *(see p50)*. ◈ *On the Capitol grounds at Maryland Ave and 1st St, SW • Map R5 • Open 10am–5pm daily • Dis. access • Free*

7 Bartholdi Park and Fountain

Another oasis for Capitol Hill visitors, this immaculate park is bursting with flowers and ornamental plants. Its symmetrical design radiates out from the fine Gilded Age cast-iron Bartholdi Fountain, a three-story high construction of supple human forms, European-style lights, and a non-stop flow of water *(see p51)*. ◈ *Independence Ave at Canal St, SW • Map R5 • Dis. access • Free*

8 Sewall-Belmont House

Built in 1750 and expanded into its current mansion size in 1800, this house is one of the most historic in Washington. It is thought that one past resident, Albert Gallatin, Treasury Secretary for Jefferson and Monroe, may have worked out the financial details of the Louisiana Purchase – which nearly doubled the size of the United States – here. The house was the only private residence burned during the War of 1812 because only from here did Americans fire on the invading British *(see p36)*. The completely rebuilt home was bought by the National Women's Party in 1929 and remains their home today. Visitors can see the elaborate but homey period furnishings of the house's past, as well as the museum's fascinating collection of objects and documents fundamental to the suffragist and feminist movements in the United States, and the oldest feminist library in the US *(see p44)*. ◈ *144 Constitution Ave, NE • Map S4 • Open 11am–3pm Tue–Fri, noon–4pm Sat • Donation*

Bartholdi Fountain

Hallway, Sewall-Belmont House

9 Capital Children's Museum

Designed to be both liberating and challenging for children, the museum touches on science, international cultures, artistic creation, and urban living in settings that children love. The firemen's garb and pole and the Metrobus cab – part of the City-scapes exhibit – are favorites (see p52). ⓢ 800 3rd St, NE • Map S3 • Open Labor Day– Memorial Day: 10am–5pm Tue–Sun; Memorial Day to Labor Day: daily • Dis. access • Adm

10 National Postal Museum

The US Postal Service delivers over 600 million items of mail every day, and this ingenious museum manages to communicate the human scale of the system. The vast airmail system, with its thousands of employees, is shown to be based on individual pilots and airplanes. An interactive display enables visitors to dive into direct marketing and mail order, even designing their own advertising piece (see p43). ⓢ 2 Massachusetts Ave, NE • Map R4 • Open 10am–5:30pm daily • Dis. access • Free

A Day Around Eastern Market

Morning

🕐 Before a day of shopping, begin with a bit of history at the **Library of Congress** (see pp24–5), a handsome example of the Italian Renaissance style, with unsurpassed interiors. The first tour is at 10:30am.

Turn right to East Capitol Street, right again, and continue one block to the **Folger Shakespeare Library and Theater** (see p71). The Elizabethan theater is enchanting, and the material displayed is both rare and fascinating.

Walk east to 7th Street and turn right. A little over two blocks farther on is **Eastern Market** (see p74). On weekends it is sur-rounded by arts and crafts vendors and flower stalls.

🍽 **The Market Lunch** (see p75) inside is a great choice for lunch.

Afternoon

If you visit the market on a Saturday, spend the afternoon at the Capitol Hill Flea Market, across the street from Eastern Market. It features 100 or more vendors selling antiques, Oriental rugs, fabrics, fine art photo-graphs, jewelry, and other items. If the flea market is closed, walk a block south of Eastern Market and visit Woven History and Silk Road (311–5 7th St, SE • Map Q4 • 202-543-1758 • Open 10am–6pm daily) for its fabrics, rugs, and crafts from Asia and South America.

To return home, turn right and the Eastern Market metro stop is straight ahead of you.

Left **Ebenezer United Methodist Church** Right **Ulysses S. Grant Memorial**

🔟 Best of the Rest

1 Eastern Market
Weekends are the time to visit to take in the crafts and farm produce stalls *(see p57)*. ◉ *7th St & North Carolina Ave, SE • Map S5*

2 Ebenezer United Methodist Church
The first congregation of African-American Methodists and Episcopals in Washington. It also became home to the first public school for black children after the Emancipation Proclamation. ◉ *420 D St, SE • Map S5 • Open 8:30am–3pm Mon–Fri • Free*

3 Ulysses S. Grant Memorial
This equestrian grouping honors the Union victory in the Civil War. Sculptor Henry Shrady (1871–1922) took 20 years to complete the work *(see p49)*. ◉ *Union Square • Map R5*

4 Emancipation Monument
Lincoln holds the Emancipation Proclamation while the last slave, Archer Alexander, breaks his chains *(see p47)*. ◉ *Lincoln Park • Metro Eastern Market*

5 Statue of Mary McLeod Bethune
This modern sculpture of the great African-American educator and activist symbolizes knowledge handed down through generations *(see p47)*. ◉ *Lincoln Park • Metro Eastern Market*

6 Frederick Douglass Museum
The home of the African-American activist contains many of his possessions, including a document proclaiming him a "freed man" signed by Lincoln *(see p47)*. ◉ *316–20 A St, NE • Map S4 • Open noon–2pm Mon, Wed & Fri • Free*

7 Christ Church
This elegant church, built in 1805, had many prominent parishioners, including presidents Madison and Monroe. ◉ *620 G St, SE • Map S6*

8 National Guard Memorial
This gallery remembers citizens who have contributed their time, and sometimes their lives, to protect the nation. ◉ *1 Massachusetts Ave, NW • Map R4 • Open 9am–4pm Mon–Fri • Dis. access*

9 Voice of America
Most of VOA's programming, broadcasting US news around the world, is created at these studios. ◉ *330 Independence Ave, SW • Map R5 • Currently closed to the public*

10 Alleys and Carriageways
The alleys of Capitol Hill were notorious in the 19th century for squalid and cramped shantylike residences. Today, those sites have been turned into charming little homes. ◉ *Map S5*

Price Categories

For a three-course meal for one with half a bottle of wine (or equivalent meal), taxes and extra charges.

$
$$
$$$
$$$$ $100
$$$$$ over $100

Left **The Market Lunch** Right **America**

Places to Eat

1 Dubliner Pub
An Irish pub with free-flowing pints and good solid food: try filet of salmon, lamb with mustard crust or the shepherd's pie. Outdoor patio in summer. Irish music from 9pm. ⊗ 520 N Capitol St, NW • Map R4 • 202-737-3773 • Dis. access • $$

2 The Market Lunch
This lunch counter with nearby tables serves barbecue food North Carolina style, with a specialty in seafood. Crabcakes, river fish, and flavorful salads. ⊗ Eastern Market • Map S5 • 202-547-8444 • No credit cards • Dis. access • $

3 America
An enormous restaurant with an enormous menu – over 100 entrées – spread over three stories of Union Station and on to a walkway in good weather. Traditional American fare, such as peanut butter and jelly sandwiches, to New American cuisine. ⊗ Union Station • Map R4 • 202-682-9555 • Dis. access • $$

4 Café Berlin
A German restaurant in a townhouse setting. Wiener schnitzel, pork loin with sauerkraut, and other hearty dishes. The desserts are tempting. ⊗ 322 Massachusetts Ave, NE • Map S4 • 202-543-7656 • Dis. access • $$

5 Bullfeathers
Popular with politicians, this bar has a better-than-average selection of salads, sandwiches, and hamburgers. Crowded at weekday lunchtimes. ⊗ 410 1st St, SE • Map R5 • 202-543-5005 • Dis. access • $$

6 La Colline
A fine, unpretentious French restaurant. Try the terrine of foie gras or rack of lamb. ⊗ 400 N Capitol St, NW • Map R4 • 202-737-0400 • Dis access • $$$

7 Chesapeake Bagel Bakery
Fresh-baked bagels with 14 kinds of cream cheese and other fillings. ⊗ 215 Pennsylvania Ave, SE • Map S5 • 202-546-0994 • $

8 Library of Congress Café
If you enjoy feeling part of the government scene, this is the place to eat. ⊗ Madison Bldg, 6th Floor, Independence Ave, SE • Map S5 • 202-707-8300 • $

9 Tortilla Coast
Great Tex-Mex food. George W. Bush was a customer before his election. ⊗ 400 1st St, SE • Map R5 • 202-546-6768 • Dis access • $

10 Union Station Food Court
Bigger than average range of national and regional food. ⊗ Union Station • Map R5 • 202-371-9441 • No credit cards • Dis access • $

Note: Unless otherwise stated, all restaurants accept credit cards and serve vegetarian meals

Left **National Museum of American History** Right **United States Holocaust Memorial Museum**

The Mall and Federal Triangle

EVEN WASHINGTONIANS WHOSE DAILY PURSUITS *rarely take them to the Mall regard this magnificent open expanse as the heart of the city. A grassy park with carefully preserved trees, the Mall stretches 2.5 miles (4 km) from the Capitol to the east to the Potomac River, just beyond the Lincoln Memorial, to the west. Alongside and nearby are the core symbols of the city and the nation: memorials to past suffering and triumphs, the workplaces of the federal government, and the Smithsonian Institution museums, entrusted with "the increase and diffusion of knowledge." The Mall also serves as a national public square – it fills to capacity for the dazzling Fourth of July celebration and fireworks display, while the Smithsonian Folklife Festival (see p64) brings food, dance, storytelling, and crafts from all over the world. And the space is enlivened daily with ordinary people jogging, strolling, or just enjoying the extraordinary views.*

Sights

1. National Mall
2. National Gallery of Art
3. National Air and Space Museum
4. National Museum of American History
5. Hirshhorn Museum and Sculpture Garden
6. National Museum of Natural History
7. United States Holocaust Memorial Museum
8. Washington Monument
9. Lincoln Memorial
10. Vietnam Veterans' Memorial

Museum of Natural History

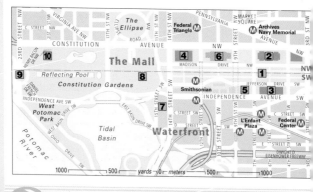

National Mall

1 Washington's first city planner, Pierre L'Enfant, envisioned a sweeping park and "a grand avenue," reaching from the Capitol westward up to "the President's House," and beyond, up 16th Street, NW. This former wilderness was put to practical use during its early history, hosting a major railroad terminal, an armory, and, during the Civil War, extensive facilities for troops, including grazing cattle for military provisions. A small zoo opened here in the 1880s, and bison replaced the cattle. Today, the area has been cleared and simplified to become a great public space with free access for all. ◈ *Map Q5*

National Gallery of Art

2 It's fun just strolling through this grand building surrounded by illustrious artworks dating from before the Renaissance to the current day. The sculpture garden is a hit with visitors for both its public art and its outdoor setting and inviting café *(see pp20–23)*.

National Air and Space Museum

3 The story of flight, one of the most stirring in human history, is dramatically depicted in this favorite museum, renowned for its collection of precious artifacts of the challenging experience of flying *(see pp16–17)*.

Central Plaza, Hirshhorn Museum

National Museum of American History

National Museum of American History

4 The story of the United States of America, from its often troubled beginnings to the present day, is told here, both through public icons and through examinations of the daily lives of ordinary people. The much-acclaimed "The American Presidency" exhibit displays engaging personal belongings of the presidents in a patriotic setting. "America on the Move" draws on the museum's unparalleled collections and looks at all the modes of transportation from 1876 to the present. There are also interactive experiences.

Hirshhorn Museum and Sculpture Garden

5 The only public gallery in the city with the sole focus on modern and up-and-coming art, this museum's holdings and exhibitions of contemporary international works are exceptional. The unusual circular building, designed by Gordon Bunschaft and completed in 1974, provides a striking setting for outdoor sculpture in the surrounding plaza. Another fine sculpture garden across Jefferson Drive displays more than 60 pieces of large-scale contemporary work *(see p40)*. ◈ *7th St, at Independence Ave, SW • Map Q5 • Open 10am–5:30pm daily • Dis. access • Free*

6 National Museum of Natural History

A favorite with children, yet filled with fascinating displays and artifacts that appeal to everyone, the vast halls of this Smithsonian museum have everything from the tiny, precisely arranged bones of a snake to a giant ritual statue from Easter Island. Other exhibits include Pacific island canoes, fabulous gemstones, a giant squid, a scene from a Chinese opera, and an Egyptian mummy case *(see p42)*.
Ⓢ *Constitution Ave & 10th St, NW*
• Map P4 • Open 10am–5:30pm daily
• Dis. access • Free

7 United States Holocaust Memorial Museum

Among the city's most challenging sites, this museum is both a working study center for issues relating to the Holocaust and a national memorial for the millions murdered by the World War II Nazi government. The museum is solemn and respectful while engrossing and highly informative. Free timed passes are required to view the three-story permanent exhibition; special exhibitions, including the child-oriented "Remember the Children: Daniel's Story" can be seen without passes *(see p42)*.
Ⓢ *100 Raoul Wallenberg Place, SW (14th St between Independence Ave & C St, SW) • Map P5 • Open 10am–5:30pm daily; Closed Yom Kippur, Dec 25 • Dis. access • Free*

8 Washington Monument

The plain Egyptian design of this radiant spire was largely the result of congressional cost-cutting, but now it seems an inspired choice. At 555 ft (165 m), the monument, built to honor the first president of the United States, towers over everything in the neighborhood. The view from the observation platform at the top, reached by a 72-second elevator ride, is unforgettable. The new elevator on the descending trip allows visitors see some of the many commemorative stones that have been laid in the masonry walls *(see p48)*. Ⓢ *15th St & Constitution Ave, NW • Map P5*
• Open 9am–5pm daily; Closed Jul 4, Dec 25 • Dis. access • Free

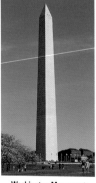

Washington Monument

9 Lincoln Memorial

This imposing marble memorial honors the US president who carried the country through its most difficult era. Designed by Henry Bacon (1866–1924) and featuring a monumental 19-ft (6-m) high statue of the seated Lincoln by Daniel Chester French (1850–1931), the

Lincoln Memorial

memorial was dedicated in 1922. The Greek architecture reflects the ideals of its time *(see p48)*.

🔊 *23rd St, NW & West Potomac Park • Map M5 • Open 8am–midnight daily*

🔟 Vietnam Veterans' Memorial

This stark remembrance features a black polished wall on which are carved the names of soldiers who died during the Vietnam War. Controversial when it opened, because of its minimalism and because it failed to glorify the war, the memorial has become one of the world's most popular. Its creator, Maya Lin, was a 21-year-old Chinese-American student when she completed the design. More traditional statues were added in 1984 *(see p48)*.

🔊 *Constitution Ave & Henry Bacon Drive, NW • Map M5 • Open 8am–midnight daily • Dis. access • Free*

Statues, Vietnam Veterans' Memorial

A Morning Walk by the Waterfront

🕐 Begin at the **Franklin D. Roosevelt Memorial** *(see p48)* on West Basin Drive. A Tourmobile stop *(see p117)* is directly in front of the memorial (parking is limited). The sweeping flow of this memorial carries visitors past waterscapes punctuated by engravings of the words of the president and evocative sculptures of his times.

On the left, leaving the memorial, is the little Japanese pagoda given to the city as a gesture of friendship by the mayor of Yokohama in 1958. Graceful Japanese cherry trees line the Tidal Basin bank beyond. Continue east across Inlet Bridge. About five minutes along the walkway stands the brilliant **Jefferson Memorial** *(see p48)*, noted for its delicate design in spite of its size. Looking out from the steps here to the city is a wonderful experience.

Continue around the waterfront, cross Outlet Bridge, and bear to the left to the little boathouse, where you can rent a paddleboat for a unique view of the Tidal Basin *(Open Mar–Apr: 10am–5pm; May–Oct: 10am–6pm • Adm)*. If you prefer to stay on dry ground, continue north toward the **Washington Monument** and cross Maine Avenue leading to Raoul Wallenberg Place. On the right is the **US Holocaust Memorial Museum**. Before taking in the exhibits, gird yourself with some kosher fare in the **Museum Café** *(see p85)*. Then spend the afternoon in remembrance of lives tragically lost under the Nazi regime.

Around Town – The Mall & Federal Triangle

Left **Arts and Industries Building** Right **National Archives façade**

Best of the Rest

1 Arts and Industries Building
Houses material from the Centennial Exposition of 1876. ◈ *900 Jefferson Drive, SW • Map Q5 • Open 10am–5:30pm daily • Dis. access • Free*

2 Enid A. Haupt Garden
These formal gardens contrast scale, color, and scent *(see p50)*. ◈ *1000 Jefferson Drive, SW • Map P5 • Open 7am–5:45pm daily • Dis. access • Free*

3 National Archives of the United States
Home to the foundation documents of the nation, including the Declaration of Independence. ◈ *7th St and Constitution Ave, NW • Map Q4 • Dis. access • Free*

4 Franklin D. Roosevelt Memorial
The inclusion of FDR's dog in the statuary lends to the human scale of this tribute *(see p48)*. ◈ *Ohio Drive, SW • Map N6 • Open 8am–midnight daily • Dis. access • Free*

5 Jefferson Memorial
Words of the Declaration of Independence are engraved on the wall here *(see p48)*. ◈ *Tidal Basin • Map N6 • Open 8am–midnight daily • Dis. access • Free*

6 National Museum of the American Indian
This museum will be a national center for Native American programs. ◈ *4th St and Independence Ave, SW • Map Q5 • Opening 2004*

7 Korean War Veterans Memorial
The 19 stainless steel sculptures in this memorial to the 1953 Korean "police action" wrenchingly evoke the realities of war. ◈ *French Drive, SW • Map M5 • Open 8am–midnight daily • Dis. access • Free*

8 Bureau of Engraving and Printing
Workers here create and print all US paper currency – 37 million notes a day worth nearly $700 million. ◈ *14th St at D St, SW • Map P5 • Tours 8am–2pm Mon–Fri • Dis. access • Free*

9 National Museum of African Art
An accessible and absorbing collection – be sure to see the pre-Colonial art of Benin. ◈ *950 Independence Ave, SW • Map Q5 • Open 10am–5:30pm daily • Dis. access • Free*

10 Old Post Office
The view from the tower here is among the finest in the city. A popular food court and shops draw hordes of visitors *(see p57)*. ◈ *12th St and Pennsylvania Ave, NW • Map P4 • Tower: open daily, hours vary (call 202-606-8691 to check); Dis. access; Free*

Left **Smithsonian Teddy Bears** Right **National Air and Space Museum store**

Items in Museum Stores

1 Smithsonian Teddy Bear
This is the Smithsonian's commemorative version of the Ideal Toy Company's 1902 bear, based on a famous *Washington Star* cartoon showing "Teddy" Roosevelt with a bear cub. In the National Museum of American History *(see pp18–19)*.

2 Compass
The Lewis and Clark expedition organized by Thomas Jefferson in 1803 was able to follow rivers much of the way, but depended on a compass like this one for guidance. Formerly in the National Museum of American History *(see pp18–19)*.

3 Ceramic Teapots
Ceramic teapots in various colors, styles, and sizes. The most popular are the decorative mini teapots. In the National Museum of Natural History *(see p77)*.

4 Dinosaurmania
The ultimate action figures, plus many genuinely informative as well as fun activities and kits, are found in the TriceraShop here in the National Museum of Natural History *(see p77)*.

5 Leather Flight Jackets
Good-quality leather jackets recreate the genuine early flying jackets, and the selection and prices are reasonable. In the National Air and Space Museum *(see pp16–17)*.

6 Wooden Figures and Tableware
These marvelous carvings capture African skill and vision in the use of wood. In the National Museum of African Art *(see p82)*.

7 Star Theater
A fun and educational simulation of the planetarium experience, capturing at least some of the excitement of the heavens. In the National Air and Space Museum *(see pp16–17)*.

8 Geodes and Fossils
The Gem and Mineral store has beautiful examples of geodes – sparkling crystals grown within hollows of other stones – and of fossils embedded in various matrixes. In the National Museum of Natural History *(see p77)*.

9 Chrysanthemum Satin Kimono
One of the many magnificent fabric creations available at these two Oriental museum stores. They also have unusual novelties such as *haiku* refrigerator magnets. In the Freer Gallery of Art and Arthur M. Sackler Gallery *(see pp40–41)*.

10 Freeze-Dried Astronaut Ice Cream
Everyone should try this at least once. It has an odd texture but it really is a dessert treat for space-farers. In the National Air and Space Museum *(see pp16–17)*.

Left **Dinosaur Hall** Center **Insect Zoo** Right **"How Things Fly"**

Children's Attractions

1 Johnson IMAX Theater
The movie screen at the Museum of Natural History is 66 ft high and 90 ft wide (20 m x 28 m), and some of the films shown are 3-D using polarized glasses. Most film subjects are hits with children *(see p78)*.

2 Smithsonian Carousel
This lovely carousel with its fancifully carved steeds is a treat even for quite young visitors. The sounds of the band organ are very cheering. ⓢ *1000 Jefferson Dr, SW • Map P5 • Open 10am–5:30pm daily weather permitting • Adm*

3 O. Orkin Insect Zoo
Live arthropods scamper and creep in this section of the Museum of Natural History – some can also be held *(see p78)*.

4 "How Things Fly"
Highly interactive exhibits and scheduled demonstrations at the National Air and Space Museum explain the principles that make flight possible. Kids can understand natural animal flight and human flight in contraptions from balloons to the space shuttle *(see pp16–17)*.

5 Children's Film Program at the National Gallery of Art
Animations, environmental and nature films, and child's-eye views of life are compiled into lively shows the right length for children's attention spans *(see pp20–23)*.

6 Skylab Orbital Workshop
Kids love Skylab in the National Air and Space Museum because visitors can walk inside and see the tools, instruments, and living facilities of the actual 1973 spacecraft, although this is the backup module that never flew in space *(see pp16–17)*.

7 Ice Skating
The fountain in the National Gallery of Art Sculpture Garden *(see p23)* is frozen for ice skating in the winter, and visitors can rent skates on site.

8 Dinosaur Hall
Many kids make their first contact with the study of the natural world through their fascination with dinosaurs. The displays at the National Museum of Natural History should wow them – the *Diplodocus longus* is 87 ft (27 m) long *(see p78)*.

9 Hands-On History Room
Historical artifacts in this room in the National Museum of American History, such as a cotton gin, are recreated and made available for children to use *(see pp18–19)*.

10 View from top of the Washington Monument
The view from the 555 ft high (170 m) monument *(see p48)* is spectacular. The ride in the elevator is interesting because high-tech windows become transparent or opaque in a wink.

Above **Old Post Office Food Court**

Price Categories

For a three-course
meal for one with half
a bottle of wine (or
equivalent meal), taxes,
and extra charges.

$	under $30
$$	$30–$50
$$$	$50–$75
$$$$	$75–$100
$$$$$	over $100

10 Places to Eat

1 Cascade Café
Behind a glass wall in the National Gallery of Art concourse is a man-made waterfall spilling over a stepped cascade. Facing this view is an attractive café with a wide range of hot and cold food. ◎ *4th St between Madison Drive & Pennsylvania Ave, NW • Map Q4 • 202-737-4215 • Dis. access • $*

2 Old Post Office Food Court
Pizza, sushi, bagels, ice cream, and cookies are sold in this interesting food court. ◎ *12th St & Pennsylvania Ave, NW • Map P4 • 202-289-4224 • No credit cards • Dis. access • $*

3 The Palm Court
This old-fashioned ice cream parlor has super desserts based on early 20th-century treats. ◎ *Museum of American History, 4th St & Constitution Ave, NW • Map P4 • 202-357-2700 • Dis. access • $*

4 Garden Café
This little restaurant in the National Gallery of Art has the choice of a good buffet or a traditional à la carte menu. Surroundings of greenery combine with lofty ceilings. ◎ *6th St and Constitution Ave, NW • Map Q4 • 202-216-2480 • Dis. access • $*

5 National Air and Space Museum
The chain restaurants McDonald's, Boston Market, and Donato's Pizzeria have taken over the greenhouse-like food service area *(see pp16–17)*.

6 Pavilion Café
Sandwiches and salads, pizzas, and a variety of desserts are served in a lively setting, with a view of skaters in season. ◎ *7th St and Madison Dr, NW • Map Q4 • 202-289-3360 • Dis. access • $*

7 United States Holocaust Memorial Museum
The Museum Café serves traditional and contemporary American favorites. Kosher meals available *(see p78)*.

8 Reagan International Trade Center Food Court
This large food court has Texas grill, sushi, and dim sum as a few of the specialties. ◎ *1300 Pennsylvania Ave, NW • Map Q4 • 202-312-1300 • Dis. access • $*

9 National Museum of American History
Standard American fare in an efficient cafeteria setting. Kids enjoy the hot dogs *(see pp18–19)*.

10 Atrium Café
The atrium of the Museum of Natural History is six stories high, and the food is also good. Live jazz played on Friday nights *(see p78)*.

> **Note:** Unless otherwise stated, all restaurants accept credit cards and serve vegetarian meals

Left **Willard Hotel** Right **US Navy Memorial**

Old Downtown

LIKE OTHER URBAN DOWNTOWN AREAS, *Washington's city center is filled with shops, hotels, restaurants, and theaters for every taste. Yet downtown Washington borders Pennsylvania Avenue – often called "America's main street." This is the direct route between the White House and the Capitol, and is therefore rich in historic associations. Presidential inauguration parades sweep down the avenue every four years; citizens protest here; President Lincoln was shot and died nearby. Washington's importance to world culture is reflected in the ease with which local restaurants and stores cater to an international clientele. Recently revitalized, the area draws visitors to the attractions of Chinatown, the MCI Center, and the feeling of being at the center of the political world.*

🔟 Sights

1. Ford's Theater
2. MCI Center
3. FBI Building
4. National Building Museum
5. National Museum of Women in the Arts
6. National Aquarium
7. Chinatown
8. Willard Hotel
9. Martin Luther King, Jr. Memorial Library
10. US Navy Memorial

FBI Building

ord's Theater

1 Ford's Theater

John Wilkes Booth shot Abraham Lincoln in a balcony box here on April 14, 1865 – a tragic event that has made Ford's Theater one of America's best-known historical sites. A museum contains Booth's .44 caliber Derringer pistol and other objects and information giving insights into Lincoln and the assassination plot. The restored building also houses a lively theater company. Directly across 10th Street is Petersen House, where Lincoln died after being carried from the theater *(see p44).* ◈ *10th St between E & F Sts, NW • Map Q4 • Open 9am–5pm daily • Dis. access • Free*

2 MCI Center

While the MCI Center is principally a sports arena, it has also become an unofficial community center. It draws crowds night after night with college and professional sports events, big-name concerts, circuses, figure skating performances, and other events *(see p52).* ◈ *601 F St, NW • Map Q4 • Dis. access*

3 Federal Bureau of Investigation Building

The FBI tour has been a favorite with visitors since it was launched in 1937. Visitors on the one-hour tour learn about the history and goals of the bureau, pass through working laboratories analyzing forensic evidence, then watch a demonstration of officers training in the use of firearms. Although tours by members of the public are no longer allowed at the time of writing, this situation may change in the future. If you would like to visit, call ahead to make enquiries. ◈ *9th & E Sts, NW • Map Q4 • Open 8:45am–4:15pm Mon–Fri • Dis. access • Free*

4 National Building Museum

This grand structure would be a fabulous place to visit even if it was empty. Its eight massive interior columns are among the largest in the world, and its immense interior space has beautiful natural light. The museum itself is dedicated to documenting and displaying important themes in the art and craft of building structures. It has permanent exhibitions on the city of Washington and on art created from tools, and mounts a stream of temporary exhibitions on topics such as the growth of urban transit and the development of architectural and construction methods. Other exhibits highlight the work of individual prominent architects. ◈ *401 F St, NW • Map Q4 • Open 10am–5pm Mon–Sat, 11am–5pm Sun • Dis. access • Free, donations appreciated.*

Great Hall, National Building Museum

National Museum of Women in the Arts

5 National Museum of Women in the Arts

The collection of works by female artists here is among the world's best, ranging from Lavinia Fontana's *Portrait of a Noblewoman* (c.1580) to Brazilian artist Frida Baranek's bristling 1991 *Untitled* (see p41). ◈ *1250 New York Ave, NW • Map P3 • Open 10am–5pm Mon–Sat, noon–5pm Sun • Dis. access • Adm*

6 National Aquarium

One of the oldest aquariums in the world (1873). Sharks, alligators, piranha, and nearly 300 other species are housed here, and there are preservation programs that help other fish in the wild (see p53). ◈ *14th St between Pennsylvania & Constitution Aves, NW • Map P4 • Open 9am–5pm daily • Dis. access • Adm*

7 Chinatown

Chinese culture abounds here, with an array of restaurants and shops. A Chinese arch was funded by Beijing and constructed in 1986, with seven pagoda-style roofs ornamented with 300 dragons. ◈ *7th & H Sts, NW • Map Q3*

8 Willard Hotel

A glorious center of historic and political Washington. Every US president, beginning with Franklin Pierce in 1853, has stayed as a guest or attended functions here. When Lincoln was inaugurated in March 1861, there were already assassination threats. Detective Alan Pinkerton smuggled him into the Willard,

Pennsylvania Avenue

When the federal government moved to the city in 1800, Pennsylvania Avenue was selected as the "main street" because the area to the south was too muddy after rains, and the avenue offered a direct route from the President's House to the Capitol – the only substantial buildings in town.

and presidential business was conducted before the fireplace the lobby. ◈ *1401 Pennsylvania Ave, NW • Map P4 • Dis. access*

9 Martin Luther King, Jr. Memorial Library

This handsome building was dedicated in 1972 as a memorial to Martin Luther King, Jr. and as a public library. In the lobby is a mural by Don Miller depicting the life of Dr. King and the achievements of the civil rights movement. ◈ *901 G St, NW • Map Q4 • Open 10am–9pm Mon–Thu, 10am–5:30p, Fri–Sat, 1–5pm Sun • Dis. access • Free*

10 US Navy Memorial

The centerpiece of this delightful public space is a granite floor – a huge map of the world surrounded by fountains. A statue, dubbed "The Lone Sailor," overlooks the expanse (see p49 A free film shows daily at noon. ◈ *7th St & Pennsylvania Ave, NW • Map Q4 • Open 9:30–5pm Mon–Sat (closed Mon, Nov–Feb) • Dis. access • Free*

Archway, Chinatown

Left **Jaleo** Right **Old Ebbitt Grill**

Price Categories

For a three-course meal for one with half a bottle of wine (or equivalent meal), taxes and extra charges.

$	under $30
$$	$30–$50
$$$	$50–$75
$$$$	$75–$100
$$$$$	over $100

10 Places to Eat

1 Willard Room
Among the most sumptuous public dining rooms in the world. Desserts are excellent. Jacket and tie required for men. ✆ 1401 Pennsylvania Ave, NW • Map P4 • 202-637-7440 • Dis. access • $$$$

2 Jaleo
A fine *tapas* restaurant, Jaleo draws raves for its eggplant flan and sautéed shrimp. The atmosphere is lively, with great music and plenty of sangria. ✆ 480 7th St, NW • Map Q4 • 202-628-7949 • Dis. access • $$

3 Old Ebbitt Grill
A pub-style restaurant with great hamburgers and seasonal entrées. Oyster bar in season. ✆ 675 15th St, NW • Map P4 • 202-347-4800 • Dis. access • $$

4 Café Atlantico
Creative Caribbean, Spanish, and Central American dishes sparkle here and the atmosphere is fun. The wine list is exceptional, and service is of very high quality. ✆ 405 8th St, NW • Map Q4 • 202-393-0812 • Dis. access • $$

5 Les Halles
A casual French steakhouse that also serves traditional bistro dishes such as cassoulet. Customers rave over the genuine French fries, and the steak, *frites*, and salad combination is great. ✆ 1201 Pennsylvania Ave, NW • Map P4 • 202-347-6848 • Dis. access • $$

6 Hard Rock Café
Stained-glass windows honor rock-and-roll greats in this world-wide chain. Mainly grilled meat, but pasta dishes are available. ✆ 999 E St, NW • Map Q4 • 202-737-ROCK • Dis. access • $

7 Full Kee
This Chinatown restaurant serves outstanding soups, assembled at an open station. ✆ 509 H St, NW • Map Q3 • 202-371-2233 • No credit cards • $

8 Red Sage
Tex-Mex food with a healthy twist. ✆ 605 14th St, NW • Map P4 • 202-638-4444 • Dis. access • $$

9 Tony Cheng's Mongolian Restaurant
Diners choose their own ingredients for a chef-prepared barbecue. ✆ 619 H St, NW • Map Q4 • 202-842-8669 • $

10 District Chophouse and Brewery
A great bar with good food, it caters to sports fans from the MCI Center. ✆ 509 7th St, NW • Map Q4 • 202-347-3434 • Dis. access • $$$

Note: Unless otherwise stated, all restaurants accept credit cards and serve vegetarian meals

Left **Organization of American States** Center **The White House** Right **Kennedy Center**

The White House and Foggy Bottom

THE MAJESTIC WHITE HOUSE CLEARLY DEFINES *this area of the city –
everyday business in Washington frequently takes place around the house
because the major east-west routes, Pennsylvania and Constitution Avenues,
are close by. Many government buildings stand in the vicinity, including the
old and new Executive Office Buildings, the Federal Reserve Building, and
the State and Treasury Departments. To the west lies Foggy Bottom, a former
swamp area now home to George Washington University. Farther west, the
Kennedy Center stands on the waterfront. Throughout the area, as one
would expect, restaurants, hotels, and shops provide the quality of service
required by high-profile diplomats and politicians.*

🔟 Sights

1. The White House
2. Kennedy Center
3. Corcoran Gallery of Art
4. Renwick Gallery
5. Old Executive Office Building
6. Treasury Building
7. Octagon
8. Organization of American States
9. Daughters of the American Revolution
10. Federal Reserve Building

Corcoran Gallery statue

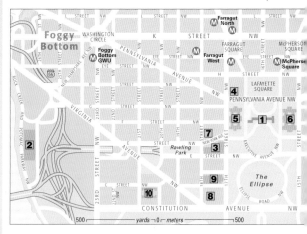

1 The White House
Beautiful from any angle and still glowing from its repainting in the 1990s, the White House is a symbol of US political power and of democracy throughout the world *(see pp12–15)*.

2 Kennedy Center
A memorial to President John F. Kennedy, this huge performance complex – the largest in the country – presents the best expressions of the artistic culture he loved so well. National and international stars perform opera, concerts, musical comedy, drama, jazz, dance, and ballet, and even experimental multimedia productions. Located overlooking the Potomac, its terraces and rooftop restaurant have dazzling views *(see p58)*. *New Hampshire Ave at Rock Creek Parkway, NW • Map M4 • Dis. access*

3 Corcoran Gallery of Art
This 1897 building is among the finest Beaux Arts designs in the United States. Note the atrium with its exquisite symmetrical stairway. The art collection inside includes some of the very best of American and European masterworks. In the American art collection, works by the Hudson River School and the Luminists are especially strong *(see p40)*. *500 17th St, NW (at New York Ave) • Map N4 • Open 10am–5pm Wed–Mon (10am–9pm Thu); guided tours noon Wed–Mon, 7:30pm Thu, 2:30pm Sat–Sun • Dis. access • Adm*

4 Renwick Gallery
This Smithsonian museum is a gem, with its displays of fine craft works. The second-floor Grand Salon served as a ballroom and site for special events when the Corcoran Gallery was located here before 1897. The

Renwick Gallery entrance detail

room has been completely refurbished and a modern lighting system installed. The 1859 structure, named after its architect, James Renwick, Jr, is a marvelous Second Empire-style building *(see p40)*. *Pennsylvania Ave at 17th St, NW • Map N3 • Open 10am–5:30pm daily • Free • Dis. access*

5 Old Executive Office Building
This is another Second Empire building, but on a mammoth scale. Many people consider its highly embellished style and daunting proportions – 300,000 sq ft (27,871 sq m) of office space on five stories – to be magnificent, but Mark Twain called it "the ugliest building in America." The Departments of State, Navy, and War were housed here on its completion in 1888. Today it is home to offices for executive branch employees and the vice president *(see p45)*. *17th St and Pennsylvania Ave, NW • Map N4 • Currently closed to the public*

Old Executive Office Building

George Washington University

For the last 50 years, GWU has been a major presence in Foggy Bottom, contributing to its diversity and filling its streets with the energy of young students. Founded as Columbian College in 1821, the school adopted its current name in 1904 to honor the wishes expressed by George Washington for the establishment of a major university in the city.

The Octagon

6 Treasury Building

The Greek-Revival style of this old building, designed in 1833, suggests a Temple of Money, and the imposing interior design confirms the seriousness with which the republic has always treated its currency. The restored Salmon P. Chase Suite and the Andrew Johnson Office reflect the gravity of official actions during and after the Civil War. The burglar-proof vault is always a hit with visitors because of the beauty of its cast-iron walls and its demonstration of the low security needs of a simpler day *(see p45)*.
◈ *1500 Pennsylvania Ave, NW • Map P4 • Currently closed to the public*

7 The Octagon

This unique and graceful building houses the oldest architecture museum in the country. The house was completed in 1801 – one of the first private residences to be built to Pierre L'Enfant's plan – and provided shelter to President James Madison and his family while workers were rebuilding the White House after its destruction during the War of

1812. The exhibitions of the museum focus especially on the early Federal period of architecture, principally from 1800 to 1830. The finest display is the restoration of the house itself, designed by William Thornton, the original architect of the US Capitol, as a second home for John Tayloe III, a wealthy friend of George Washington *(see p45)*
◈ *1799 New York Ave • Map N4 • Open 10am–4pm Tue–Sun • Adm • Dis. access*

8 Organization of American States

The OAS's beautiful building, with its three round-topped arches, is one of the area's architectural delights. The OAS Art Museum of the Americas has a permanent collection of Western Hemisphere art that is one of the most important in the US. The Organization of American States is a cooperative association of all 35 countries of the hemisphere to promote economic development, protect human rights, and strengthen democracy. ◈ *17th St at Constitution Ave, NW • Map N4 • Museum: 201 18th St NW; Open 10am–5pm Tue–Sun • Free*

Liberty Bell, Treasury Building

9 Daughters of the American Revolution

The largest concert hall in the city is in Constitution Hall, the grand performance space operated by the Daughters of the American Revolution (DAR). The cornerstone of this John Russell Pope design was laid in 1928, using the same trowel George Washington used for the US Capitol building cornerstone in 1793. The DAR also has a fascinating museum of early American artifacts, ranging from a simple 17th-century dwelling to an elaborate Victorian parlor. The DAR is a patriotic organization that fosters understanding and respect for the heritage of the United States. ◎ *D St and 18th St, NW • Map N4 • Museum: Open 8:30am–4pm Mon–Fri, 1pm–5pm Sun • Free*

10 Federal Reserve Building

Another gleaming white design by Paul P. Cret, architect of the Folger Shakespeare Library *(see p71)*. The Federal Reserve System is the central banking authority in the United States, regulating and facilitating both banking and the flow of currency and financial transactions. ◎ *C St between 20th and 21 Sts, NW • Map N4*

Federal Reserve Building

A Day Exploring 17th Street NW

Morning

Begin your day with a tour of **Decatur House** *(see p45)*, a gorgeous Neo-Classical mansion. After the tour, turn left and walk to the end of the block; turn left onto 17th St, NW, and continue one block to Pennsylvania Ave. The **Renwick Gallery** *(see p91)* is on the corner. Don't miss the luxurious ballroom on the second floor.

Continuing east on Pennsylvania, you can view the renowned north portico of **The White House** *(see pp12–15)* on your right. Reverse direction, return to 17th St, and turn left to take in the remarkably ornate **Old Executive Office Building** *(see p91)*.

A block south is the **Corcoran Gallery of Art** *(see p91)* with its superb American and European art. Have lunch at the **Café des Artistes** *(see p97)*, in its Beaux Arts atrium.

Afternoon

After leaving the Corcoran, turn right and continue down 17th Street one block, to D Street. Turn right, and almost at the end of the block is the entrance of the **Daughters of the American Revolution**. In addition to the fascinating period rooms, the gift shop is a treat for anyone with an interest in quilting, samplers, or porcelain.

End your day by hailing a taxi on 17th Street to the **Kennedy Center** *(see p91)* and enjoy dinner at the **Roof Terrace Restaurant** *(see p97)*, with its stunning river views.

Around Town – Around The White House & Foggy Bottom

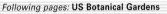

Following pages: US Botanical Gardens

Left **Benedict Arnold** Right **Watergate Senate Commitee**

Political Scandals

1 Benedict Arnold
Arnold, in the early years of the Revolution, was an effective military leader on the colonists' side. Yet, driven by money, he conspired to turn over to the British the army installation at West Point. His name became synonymous with "traitor."

2 Thomas Jefferson and Sally Hemings
The press commented in the early 1800s that Jefferson had had an affair and borne children with his slave, Sally Hemings. Jefferson denied the accusations, but now DNA evidence makes the connection probable.

3 Andrew Jackson and the Petticoat Affair
Margaret Eaton, wife of President Jackson's secretary of war, was rumored to have had a scandalous past. Jackson defended her honor and his enemies attacked, threatening his presidency.

4 "Boss" Shepherd
Alexander Shepherd pushed the Board of Public Works to great accomplishments in the 1870s, but he was later run out of town for bankrupting city government.

5 Whiskey Ring
In 1875 it was revealed that liquor taxes were being evaded by distillers and the officials they bribed. There were 110 convictions. President Grant secured the acquittal of his private secretary.

6 Teapot Dome
The oil fields at Teapot Dome, Wyoming, had been set aside as a reserve for the US Navy. In the 1920s, oil interests bribed government officials to lease the land to them, without competitive bidding.

7 Watergate
In 1972, President Nixon's re-election workers broke into the Democrats' Watergate offices planning to gather campaign information. Their arrest, and the effort to contain the scandal, forced Nixon to resign in 1974.

8 Wilbur Mills and Fanne Fox
Mills, chairman of the powerful House Ways and Means Committee, was caught frolicking with his friend, the stripper Fanne Fox. He was forced to resign in 1974.

9 Iran-Contra Affair
In the 1980s, Ronald Reagan's administration carried out plans to secretly sell US weapons to Iran and use the proceeds to support Nicaraguan rebels. The investigation revealed deception and corruption.

10 Bill Clinton and Monica Lewinsky
Clinton's denial of sexual relations with the White House intern led to charges of perjury, obstruction of justice, and an investigation by the House of Representatives.

Price Categories

For a three-course meal for one with half a bottle of wine (or equivalent meal), taxes and extra charges.	
$	under $30
$$	$30–$50
$$$	$50–$75
$$$$	$75–$100
$$$$$	over $100

Left **Galileo** Right **Kinkead's**

10 Places to Eat

1 Obelisk
Inspired market-driven menus in a relaxed atmosphere. The kitchen prepares a four- or five-course fixed-price menu, grounded in classic Italian cuisine but with a contemporary focus. ◈ 2029 P St, NW • Map N2 • 202-872-1180 • Closed Sun, Mon • $$$

2 Galileo
Exceptional modern Italian food. The kitchen has a small demonstration cooking area, where chefs prepare a tasting menu in view of the diners. ◈ 1110 21st St, NW • Map M3 • 202-293-7191 • Dis. access • $$$

3 Kinkead's
New American cooking with an emphasis on fresh seafood. The cooking is known for the careful harmonizing of flavors. ◈ 2000 Pennsylvania Ave NW • Map N3 • 202-296-7700 • Dis. access • $$$$

4 Georgia Brown's
Southern cooking with very generous portions of both food and attention. Chicken, fish, stews, corn bread, and shrimp and grits highlight the menu. ◈ 950 15th St, NW • Map P4 • 202-393-4499 • Dis. access • $$$

5 Legal Sea Foods
A chain seafood restaurant that prides itself on obtaining the best ingredients. Mahi-mahi and fried rice and seafood ravioli are popular. ◈ 2020 K St, NW • Map N3 • 202-496-1111 • Dis. access • $$$

6 Oodles Noodles
Delicious Asian noodle dishes combined with meat or vegetable concoctions. ◈ 1120 19th St, NW • Map N3 • 202-293-3138 • Dis. access • $

7 Primi Piatti
A northern Italian restaurant with fine lamb dishes and other staples. ◈ 2013 I St, NW • Map N3 • 202-223-3600 • $$

8 Roof Terrace Restaurant
At the Kennedy Center (see p91), this elegant restaurant has unrivaled views. Try sea bass with horseradish or venison with sweet potato. ◈ New Hampshire Ave at Rock Creek Parkway, NW • Map M4 • 202-416-8555 • Dis. access • $

9 Prime Rib
Steaks and chops dominate, but seafood and a vegetable platter also served. ◈ 2020 K St, NW • Map N3 • 202-466-8811 • Dis. access • $

10 Café des Artistes
In the atrium of the Corcoran Gallery (see p91). Sunday brunch with live gospel music. ◈ 17th St & New York Ave, NW • Map N4 • 202-639-1700 • Dis. access • $

Note: Unless otherwise stated, all restaurants accept credit cards and serve vegetarian meals

Left **Tudor Place** Center **M Street** Right **Grace Church**

Georgetown

*WHEN ABIGAIL ADAMS ARRIVED IN WASHINGTON in 1800, she describe•
Georgetown as "the very dirtiest hole I ever saw." Then a major port
with a huge slave and tobacco trade, cheap housing, and commercial
wharves, the town may have been unattractive. But the Chesapeake and
Ohio Canal and its competitor, the Baltimore and Ohio Railroad, brought
prosperity to Georgetown, and therefore style. When the canal began to fail
after flood damage, slum conditions returned, until Franklin D. Roosevelt
partly rehabilitated the area. Its current modish position stems from the Kenne•
era, when Georgetown became fashionable.*

Georgetown University

Sights

1. **Dumbarton Oaks Museum and Gardens**
2. **Washington Harbor**
3. **Chesapeake and Ohio Canal**
4. **M Street and Wisconsin Avenue**
5. **N Street**
6. **Georgetown University**
7. **Grace Church**
8. **Old Stone House**
9. **Tudor Place**
10. **Oak Hill Cemetery**

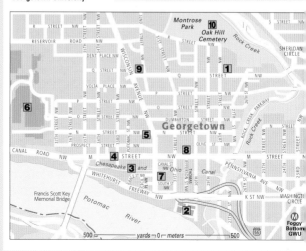

owhouses, C&O Canal

Dumbarton Oaks Museum and Gardens

This elegant Federal-style house, with its Philip Johnson-designed wing, houses a world-renowned collection of Byzantine and pre-Columbian artifacts. El Greco's *Visitation* is here also, possibly the Spanish master's last painting. The house and museum are surrounded by acres of gorgeous landscaping *(see p50)*. ◎ *1703 32nd St, NW • Map L2 • Open –5pm Tue–Sun • Adm*

Washington Harbor

Dockside cafés, good restaurants, lovely views of the Potomac and the Kennedy Center, the Watergate complex, and the Thompson boathouse, walkways for strolling, and benches for resting make the harbor a magnet for Georgetowners on warm evenings. The Washington Harbor residential and commercial building is an architectural exuberance designed by Arthur Cotton Moore and Associates. ◎ *3000–20 K St, NW, at the bottom of Thomas Jefferson St, NW (between 30th & 1st Sts) • Map L3*

Elegant Georgetown House

Chesapeake and Ohio Canal

Like so many features of the area, the C&O Canal grew from a dream of George Washington's as a gateway to commerce with the US lands to the west ("west" meaning Ohio at the time). Coal, flour, fur, timber, whiskey, iron ore, and other goods traveled on barges, towed by mules walking along canalside paths. The canal's commercial days are over, but its entire length from Georgetown to Maryland has been turned into one of the most beloved national parks. Visitors can experience the beauty and serenity of the canal by walking about a block south from M Street, NW and turning west onto the towpath. The National Park Service Visitor Center for the C&O has terrific guidance for enjoying the canal. Guided tours and mule-powered barge rides on the canal are offered *(see p51)*. ◎ *Visitor Center: 1057 Thomas Jefferson St, NW • Map L3 • Open 9am–4:30pm Wed–Sun*

M Street and Wisconsin Avenue

This intersection is surrounded by the main shopping, entertainment, dining, and bar-crawling areas of Georgetown. The attractive shops of Georgetown Park *(see p56)* include hundreds of retailers selling cool urban clothes, jewelry, fine wine, art and antiques, and countless other specialties. Restaurant food of every description is available, from modern gourmet to street window kebabs. ◎ *Map L2*

Metro Connection

Georgetown has no Metrorail station, and it used to be difficult for visitors to get to attractions, shops, and restaurants here without a long walk (20 minutes or more) from the nearest stations or a taxi ride. The Georgetown Metro Connection has been created to alleviate the problem. Running every 10 minutes daily, the shuttle bus provides inexpensive and convenient transportation to 13 locations, and, best of all, no parking worries.

5 N Street

Little attractions and oddities abound on this street, which is noted for its exemplary architecture. Best seen from the sidewalk on 28th Street, NW, the house at No. 2726 has an outstanding mosaic by Marc Chagall, a friend of the former owner. The elegant Federal house at No. 3038 was home to Ambassador Averill Harriman, who lent the house to Jacqueline Kennedy after her husband's assassination. She later bought the elaborate 1794 Thomas Beall house across the street. Lessons

N Street house

in 19th-century architecture can be learned from the Federal houses at Nos. 3327 and 3339, the Second-Empire home at No. 3025–7, and the Victorian homes of Wheatley Row at Nos. 3041–45. ◈ Map L2

6 Georgetown University

This venerable institution sits on its hill overlooking Georgetown and the Potomac like a medieval citadel, its stone towers seemingly brooding with age. Yet the university is one of the most progressive in the country. Among the many interesting buildings here is the 1875 Healy Hall, built in an elaborate Flemish Renaissance style with surprising spiral adornment. Visitors can obtain campus maps and suggestions for strolls from the booth at the main gates. ◈ Gatehouse visitors booth: O & 37th sts, NW • Map K2 • Opening hours vary depending on the university schedule. Call for details: 202-687-3600.

7 Grace Church

The 1866 church construction was built to house a congregation founded to serve the boatmen and support staff of the C&O Canal. The simple but extremely elegant design brings back the mid-19th century, although admittedly without the raucous bustle that must have accompanied the canal at its peak. The grounds are beautifully peaceful. The church offers poetry readings, theater performances, and concerts. Today's congregation has a serious devotion to community service and outreach. ◈ 1041 Wisconsin Ave, NW (one block south of M St) • Map L3 • Open by appt (tel: 202-333-7100) • Office: Open 10am–4pm Mon, Tue, & Fri • Free

For information on the Metro Connection, visit www. georgetowndc.com/shuttle.php or telephone 202-625-RIDE

Old Stone House

8 Old Stone House

This remarkable residence dating from 1766 looks a little incongruous standing directly in the heart of the shopping area, but it provides a captivating window into 18th-century life. The National Park Service provides tours and fascinating demonstrations of the crafts and tasks of colonial families. ⊗ 3051 M St • Map L2 • Open 9am–5pm Wed–Sun • Dis. access • Free

9 Tudor Place

This house museum would be remarkable for its beauty even without its historic interest. Completed in 1816, the house was built by Thomas Peter, son of a Georgetown tobacco merchant, and Martha Custis Peter, granddaughter of Martha Washington. The Peter family occupied the house for six generations and provided hospitality to many prominent guests. The formal gardens are exceptional. ⊗ 1644 31st St, NW • Map L2 • 202-965-0400 • Tours 10am, 11:30am, 1pm, 2:30pm Tue–Fri, 10am–3pm Sat, noon–3pm Sun; Closed Jan • Dis. access • Adm

10 Oak Hill Cemetery

The cemetery has a great diversity of graves and mausoleums in a Victorian garden setting. Its Gothic Revival chapel and the Van Ness Mausoleum are on the National Register of Historic Places. ⊗ R & 30th sts, NW • Map L1 • Open 10am–4pm daily

A Morning in Georgetown

Begin at **Washington Harbour** (see p99) for its views of the Potomac right on the waterfront. Take a pleasant stroll along the river before heading up Thomas Jefferson Street, NW to the National Park Service Visitor Center for the **Chesapeake and Ohio Canal** (see p99). In summer, mule-drawn barge rides are offered, with expert guides painting the historic background of the scenes before you.

Turn right and continue up Thomas Jefferson Street a short block and cross M Street, NW. In front of you is the **Old Stone House**, which has been lovingly preserved. National Park Service interpreters recreate some of the daily activities that might have taken place in the house in the 18th century.

Reverse direction and return down Thomas Jefferson Street to the canal. Turn right onto the towpath and stroll for two blocks until you reach an opening in the embankment. Follow the steps to the right to Wisconsin Avenue, NW. Cross the street to **Grace Church**. Enjoy the view of the lovely little church built for the spiritual needs of workers on the canal. The grounds, with their mature trees, make a relaxing rest spot. Recross Wisconsin Avenue and the canal to the shops at **Georgetown Park** (see p104).

Before an afternoon of retail therapy, enjoy lunch at **Clyde's of Georgetown** (see p105) on level 3 or snack from the food court on level 1.

Following pages: Georgetown rowhouses

Left & Center **Dean & Deluca** Right **Window shopping, Georgetown**

10 Places to Shop

1 The Shops at Georgetown Park

In this large indoor mall right on the canal, shoppers can find the expected fashions, but also electrical goods, luggage, and many other specialties. There is a food court and popular restaurants *(see p56)*. ◈ *3222 M St, NW • Map L2 • Dis. access*

2 Dean & DeLuca

The New York-originated gourmet food store is about as luxurious as a grocery store can get. The salad bar is superb, and the ready-made meals have brought success to countless Georgetown dinner parties.
◈ *3276 M St, NW • Map L2 • Dis. access*

3 Appalachian Spring

This shop might as well be an informal museum, considering the quality of many of the hand-made crafts for sale. The quilts, carved wood, pottery, and fabrics would grace any setting. ◈ *1415 Wisconsin Ave, NW • Map L2*

4 Britches

Britches has its own brand of natural-fiber dressy and casual clothes for men and sells brands by leading makers. ◈ *1247 Wisconsin Ave, NW • Map L2*

5 Commander Salamander

More extreme fashions for young people – Goths especially. Also serious boots and shoes, and see-through backpacks.
◈ *1420 Wisconsin Ave, NW • Map L2*

6 Georgetown Flea Market

There are some usual flea-market items here, but its reputation for selling high-quality furniture, antiques, and decorative items has increased in recent years. Sundays only.
◈ *Wisconsin Ave and S St, NW • Map L2*

7 Urban Outfitters

Casual city clothing is the staple product here. The store has its own good-quality brand of clothes. Other "urban" items, from aromatherapy candles to kitsch decorations, are stocked intermittently. ◈ *3111 M St, NW • Map L2*

8 F.A.O. Schwarz

The local branch of the famous toy bazaar. The radio-controlled PT Cruiser was a recent hit, and the jumbo music blocks are almost as big as a toddler. ◈ *3222 M St, NW • Map L2*

9 Beyond Comics II

Countless wares, fascinating for all ages, fill this shop. Not just comics but also action figures, T-shirts, posters, cards, and novelties. ◈ *3060 M St, NW • Map L2*

10 Up Against the Wall

More fashionable clothing – some for clubbing but much suitable for street wear and even business. The store sets a contemporary music theme for shoppers, and even has a part-time DJ. ◈ *3219 M St, NW • Map L2*

Price Categories

For a three-course meal for one with half a bottle of wine (or equivalent meal), taxes and extra charges.

$	under $30
$$	$30–$50
$$$	$50–$75
$$$$	$75–$100
$$$$$	over $100

Left **1789** Right **Sequoia**

Places to Eat

1 Citronelle
Chef Michel Richard is famous for his innovative dishes. Described as French/Californian, the menu has such items as scallops with fruit and tomato saffron emulsion *(see p63).*
🕲 *3000 M St, NW • Map L2 • 202-625-2150 • Dis. access • $$$$$*

2 1789
Excellent American food. The elegant townhouse is divided into five themed rooms, and was popular with President Clinton *(see p63).* 🕲 *1226 36th St, NW • Map K2 • 202-965-1789 • $$$*

3 Sequoia
Famous for its beautiful views and outdoor deck, this is a haven for people-watching as well. The American cuisine, emphasizing seafood, enhances the setting. 🕲 *3000 K St, NW • Map L3 • 202-944-4200 • Dis. access • $$*

4 Zed's Ethiopian Cuisine
The large Ethiopian population in the city has produced a number of fine restaurants; this one is rated among the best. Delicious vegetarian dishes, as well as spicy meat and poultry. 🕲 *1201 28th St, NW • Map L2 • 202-333-4710 • $*

5 Clyde's of Georgetown
This long-time Georgetown favorite trucks in local produce and incorporates it into special menu items. 🕲 *3236 M St, NW • Map L2 • 202-333-9180 • Dis. access • $*

6 Japan Inn
The restaurant's large space and fine service have kept this Japanese steakhouse popular. Teriyaki, sashimi, tempura, and steak. 🕲 *1715 Wisconsin Ave, NW • Map L2 • 202-337-3400 • Dis. access • $$*

7 Bistro Français
Unpretentious French dishes such as lamb steak with herb butter. 🕲 *3128 M St, NW • Map L2 • 202-338-3830 • Dis. access • $$*

8 Blues Alley
Billed as "the nation's finest jazz and supper club." The food includes steak, shrimp, and pasta. Reservations essential *(see p62).* 🕲 *1073 Wisconsin Ave, NW • Map L2 • 202-337-4141 • $$*

9 Daily Grill
A Californian chain serving diner-type food. 🕲 *1310 Wisconsin Ave, NW • Map L2 • 202-337-4900 • $*

10 Miss Saigon
Vegetarian specials, as well as Vietnamese stir-fries, and curries. 🕲 *3057 M St, NW • Map L2 • 202-333-5545 • $20 • Dis. access • $$*

Left **Mount Vernon** Right **Bethesda**

Beyond the City Center

THE MONUMENTAL CORE OF WASHINGTON, D.C. *is so rich in sights that visitors may be tempted to look no farther. But many delights lie within easy reach of the city center. The Michigan Avenue NE area near North Capitol Street is home to the stunning Basilica of the National Shrine of the Immaculate Conception; the U Street NW corridor is a historic town center for the African-American community; Bethesda is filled with every kind of restaurant; the Southwest waterfront is busy with commercial fishing activity; while Old Town Alexandria has a beautifully restored downtown area and fine galleries.*

🔟 Sights

1. National Cathedral
2. Arlington Cemetery
3. Mount Vernon
4. Old Town Alexandria
5. Basilica of the National Shrine of the Immaculate Conception
6. U Street, NW
7. Southwest Waterfront
8. Bethesda, Maryland
9. Great Falls
10. National Air and Space Museum Steven F. Udvar-Hazy Center

National Cathedral

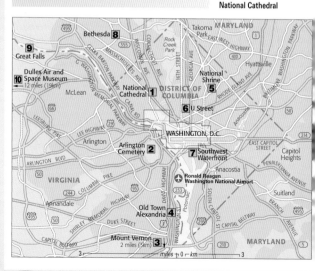

1 National Cathedral
This noble hand-crafted church is so faultless that the cathedral seems to have belonged on its elevated site forever *(see pp26–7)*.

2 Arlington Cemetery
A visit to this solemn burial ground brings conflicting emotions – pride in the determination of defenders of freedom, pleasure in the presence of its great beauty, but dismay at the loss of so many lives marked by the arrays of headstones *(see pp30–31)*.

3 Mount Vernon
Without a doubt the finest current view of George Washington the man, and of the agrarian plantation life that was an important stream leading to the revolutionary break with Great Britain *(see pp32–5)*.

4 Old Town Alexandria
This lovely old city center, across the Potomac just beneath the capital, retains the charm and hospitality of its illustrious past while giving visitors all modern conveniences, including a metro station (King Street on the yellow and blue lines). Alexandria is noted for its historical and archeological museums, Gadsby's Tavern *(see*

Altar, Basilica of the National Shrine of the Immaculate Conception

p44), the evocative system of Civil War forts and defenses at Fort Ward, and its captivating residential architecture, civilized shops, and restaurants. ◈ *Map D5*

5 Basilica of the National Shrine of the Immaculate Conception
This mammoth basilica, dedicated in 1959, incorporates more than 60 chapels and oratories that retell the diverse history of the Roman Catholic Church in the United States. Conceived in the grand style – it is the largest Roman Catholic church in the western hemisphere – the building combines Byzantine and Romanesque features, creating an intensely decorative but substantial effect. The interior is simply overwhelming in its grandeur, whatever your faith. There is also a cafeteria on the site, which is convenient because there are few nearby restaurants. ◈ *400 Michigan Ave, NE • Map D3 • Open Nov–Mar: 7am–6pm daily; Apr–Oct 7am–7pm daily • Dis. access*

Lee-Fendall House Museum, Old Alexandria

National Cathedral Schools

Like a medieval cathedral, National Cathedral is surrounded by some of the most prestigious prep schools in the city. St. Albans' alumni include Al Gore, Jesse Jackson, Jr., and broadcast journalist Brit Hume. The all-girls National Cathedral School is alma mater to a number of Rockefellers and Roosevelts. Sidwell Friends School, just up Wisconsin Avenue, educated Chelsea Clinton, the Nixon daughters, and Nancy Davis Reagan.

Duke Ellington Mural, U Street

6 U Street, NW

For much of the 20th century, U Street, NW was the main street of this bustling and prosperous African-American neighborhood. Opened as a movie theater in 1922, the Lincoln Theater (see p59) has now been refurbished and presents performances of every kind. Next door is the famous Ben's Chili Bowl, turning out great simple food for capacity crowds. The legendary jazz musician Duke Ellington (see p47) played his first paid performance at True Reformer Hall at the junction of 12th and U Street, NW. The poignant sculpture and plaza of the African-American Civil War Memorial (see p49) commemorates African-Americans who served in the Civil War. ✎ Map N1

7 Southwest Waterfront

This is a wonderful place for strolling, summer and winter. The diversity of Washington is on parade, the sailboats, yachts, and houseboats are picturesque, and the seafood – both cooked and raw – at the Southwest Fish Wharf is a showcase of what's best in eastern waters. The Fish Wharf is the current raucous embodiment of colorful markets that have flourished here continuously since about 1790. It is famed for its crabs, oysters, and clams, and also specializes in river fish not widely available elsewhere, such as perch and bass. ✎ Water St, SW • Map D4

8 Bethesda, Maryland

Locally, Bethesda is best known for its enormous quantity and range of restaurants, most of them clustered into a lively downtown area that still retains the atmosphere of a traditional town center. The high-end employment offered by Bethesda's world-renowned biotechnology industry, however, has also generated a spirited music, performance, and arts scene catering to its cultured and wealthy residents. The city is especially strong on public art. Its streets and parks spotlight distinguished contemporary works in every style, by way of sculpture and stunning painted murals. ✎ Map C2

Mural, Bethesda Avenue

Great Falls

9 Great Falls

About 15 miles (24 km) north of Washington, D.C., the Potomac is rent by magnificent waterfalls over the crags and sluices of the eroded river bed. In the state of Virginia, Great Falls Park is reached from Old Dominion Drive (Route 738). It provides spectacular overlooks above the river, fine hiking trails, and the ruins of a small 19th-century town. On the Maryland side, the Great Falls area is part of the C&O Canal *(see p99)*. The Great Falls Tavern Visitor Center offers canal rides, hiking, and ranger-led tours and remarkable river views from the overlook on Olmstead Island. ◈ Map A2 • Great Falls Tavern Visitor Center: 11710 MacArthur Blvd • Open dawn–dusk daily

10 National Air and Space Museum Steven F. Udvar-Hazy Center

This new display and restoration center for some of the museum's magnificent collection of the artifacts of flight *(see pp16–17)* is scheduled to open in December 2003 near Dulles International Airport. Two giant hangars with accompanying support buildings will provide over 760,000 sq ft (70,611 sq m) of much needed extra display space. ◈ South of main terminal at Dulles International Airport, near intersection of rtes 28 & 50

A Day in Old Town Alexandria

Morning

Begin at Christ Church *(118 N Washington St • Open 9am–4pm Mon–Sat, 2–4pm Sun • Donation)*, a handsome Georgian-style building completed in 1773. George Washington's box pew has been preserved. Then turn right onto Cameron Street toward the harbor. Continue three blocks and turn right onto North Royal Street. The two buildings on your right comprise **Gadsby's Tavern Museum** *(see p44)*. The half-hour tours are a fascinating introduction to colonial life in the city.

Head back to the harbor, turn left just before the Chart House Restaurant, and continue a half block to the Torpedo Factory Food Pavilion, with its Italian and Oriental specialties, and coffee bar. Take-out food can be eaten on the Pavilion's deck with its river views, or, a few steps upriver, in the lush Founder's Park.

Afternoon

Heading out of the Food Pavilion, directly ahead is the ticket booth for the Potomac Riverboat Company, which operates the *Admiral Tilp*. It provides a narrated 40-minute tour of the waterfront and nearby points of interest.

To the right of the tour boat kiosk is the **Torpedo Factory** *(see p112)*. It takes at least an hour for even a quick inspection of the studios of the over 164 artists here, so take a leisurely late afternoon deciding which piece you'd like to take home.

Around Town – Beyond the City Center

Following pages: **Mural in Anacostia**

Left **Capitol Coin and Stamp** Right **Logo, Torpedo Factory Art Center**

🔟 Shops

1 ADC Map and Travel Center
Maps and travel guides detail everything from the streets of Jakarta to the interstates of Iowa. Many are beautiful in themselves, and all are practical.
Ⓢ *1636 I (Eye) St, NW • Map N3*

2 Old Print Gallery
The gallery presents a huge collection of fine art prints arranged by themes. An outstanding source for political cartoons, city views, sporting prints, and historical subjects.
Ⓢ *1220 31st St, NW • Map L1*

3 Politics and Prose
A bookstore with a large selection of works on politics, culture, and government. A cheerful place, despite its serious selection, with a coffee bar.
Ⓢ *5015 Connecticut Ave, NW • Map H2*

4 Capitol Coin and Stamp
The shop has a huge variety of coins and stamps – in a correspondingly huge price range. For non-specialists, the colorful political campaign stamps, buttons, and posters will be of interest. Ⓢ *1100 17th St, NW • Map N3*

5 Affrica
This Dupont Circle gallery specializes in authentic African artifacts of the finest quality. The fabrics are astonishing in design and execution. Masks, sculptures, and jewelry are equally fine.
Ⓢ *2010 R St, NW • Map N1*

6 Torpedo Factory Art Center
The building was originally a factory to manufacture torpedoes. Today, the site contains 83 studios where artists and craftspeople create work and offer it for sale on site. Prints, ceramics, photography, painting, and sculpture.
Ⓢ *105 N Union St, Alexandria • Map D5*

7 Sutton Place Gourmet
The gourmet ingredients here are of extraordinary quality, and the selection is astonishing. The wine choice is excellent.
Ⓢ *3201 New Mexico Ave, NW • Map G4*

8 Sullivan's Toy Store
There is such a range of playthings here that it is as fascinating for adults as for children. The real stars are the items with a link to the past: model kits, craft supplies, board games, and kites. Ⓢ *3412 Wisconsin Ave, NW • Map G4*

9 Copenhaver
In Washington there remains an appreciation of the formalities of communication. Copenhaver sells the tools: elegant writing paper, envelopes, and pens.
Ⓢ *1301 Connecticut Ave, NW • Map N1*

10 Kron Chocolatier
This store is famous for its molded chocolate items – bears, sports cars, even the US Capitol. They also sell greeting cards made of chocolate. Ⓢ *Mazza Galleria, 5300 Wisconsin Ave, NW • Map G2*

Around Town – Beyond the City Center

 Browse the Torpedo Factory website at www.torpedofactory.org for their unique arts and crafts.

Price Categories

For a three-course	**$** under $30
meal for one with half	**$$** $30–$50
a bottle of wine (or	**$$$** $50–$75
equivalent meal), taxes	**$$$$** $75–$100
and extra charges.	**$$$$$** over $100

10 Places to Eat

1 Ristorante Terrazza
The northern Italian food here is creative without being radical: calamari; garlic-crusted red snapper; home-made pasta; *tiramisù*. On the second floor of the office building over the Friendship Heights Metro stop, it has an outdoor terrace for warm evenings. 🅝 *2 Wisconsin Circle, Chevy Chase, MD • Map G2 • 301-951-9292 • Dis. access • $$$*

2 Austin Grill
The inexpensive Tex-Mex food here is a cut above similar places. Even the tortilla chips are flavorful. *Tacos, enchiladas,* and *burritos,* of course, but also good grilled fish and shrimp. 🅝 *7278 Woodmont Ave, Bethesda, MD • Map C2 • 301-656-1366 • Dis. access • $*

3 Bacchus Restaurant
The *mezze* at this Lebanese restaurant are delicious. Marinated chicken, eggplant, hummus, and squid fill numerous little dishes with flavor. 🅝 *7945 Norfolk Ave, Bethesda, MD • Map C2 • 301-657-1722 • Dis. access • $$*

4 South Beach Café
The vivid and spirited atmosphere of Miami is the inspiration for this restaurant and menu: coconut shrimp; tamarind-glazed duck; and scallops with papaya and leeks. The setting is attractive, with multicolored seating, and stylized paintings. 🅝 *7904 Woodmont Ave, Bethesda, MD • Map C2 • 301-718-9737 • Dis. access • $$*

5 La Ferme
A French-American restaurant that makes imaginative use of ingredients, such as quail with Parmesan risotto. In an old farmhouse with wood beams. 🅝 *7101 Brookville Rd, Chevy Chase, MD • Map C2 • 301-986-5255 • Dis. access • $$*

6 Green Papaya
At this Vietnamese restaurant, lemon grass beef and chicken are popular. 🅝 *4922 Elm St, Bethesda, MD • Map C2 • 301-654-8986 • $$*

7 Bilbo Baggins Restaurant
The menu fuses dishes from around the world. Try crêpes with ham mousse and Gruyère. 🅝 *208 Queen St, Alexandria, VA • Map D5 • 703-683-0300 • Dis. access • $$*

8 Café Monti
Dishes from Italy and Austria: pizza; *osso bucco; Wiener schnitzel;* goulash. Place orders at a counter and find a table. 🅝 *3250 Duke St, Alexandria, VA • Map D5 • 703-370-3632 • $$*

9 Virginia Beverage Company
This working brewery serves a hearty menu. The mixed grill is excellent. 🅝 *607 King St, Alexandria, VA • Map D5 • 703-684-5397 • $$*

10 Los Amigos Restaurant
Mexican food in a relaxed atmosphere. The outdoor tables and sangria are a treat in warm weather. 🅝 *703 King St, Alexandria, VA • Map D5 • 703-548-8078 • $*

Note: Unless otherwise stated, all restaurants accept credit cards and serve vegetarian meals

STREETSMART

WASHINGTON, D.C.'S TOP 10

Left **Greyhound bus** Right **Amtrak reception desk**

Getting to Washington, D.C.

1 By Air from North America

Three airports serve Washington – Reagan Washington National, Dulles International, and Baltimore/Washington International. Twenty-four US, Canadian, and regional airlines have flights to one or more of these. For downtown Washington, Reagan is the airport of choice. ◈ *Reagan National (DCA): 703-417-8000 • Dulles International (IAD): 703-572-2700, www.metwash airports.com • Baltimore/ Washington International (BWI): 800-I-FLY-BWI, www. bwiairport.com/index.html.*

2 By Air from Europe

Most major European airlines serve Dulles, either direct or by changing planes in New York or Boston. These include Air France, British Midland, KLM, Lufthansa, SAS, and Virgin. British Airways also serves BWI.

3 By Air from Australasia

Air Canada provides a service via Halifax to Sydney; Qantas and American Airlines fly via Los Angeles. Connections are available from any of the D.C. airports.

4 By Air from Central and South America

Grupo Taca has flights between more than 40 cities in 19 countries in North, Central, and South America. United and American Airlines have routes between Washington and Central and South America, via Miami.

5 Ronald Reagan Washington National Airport

The layout of this airport is a long walkway with a semicircular bend at the end – use the shuttle bus that stops at marked locations. A Metrorail stop is right outside the northern terminals. Taxi service from the airport to the National Mall is about 10 minutes and costs around $10. The SuperShuttle provides transit to Union Station.

6 Dulles International Airport

The terminal consists of a main building and two midfield concourses reached by shuttles. The Washington Flyer coach provides transportation to the West Falls Church Metrorail station. One-way taxi fares to the city are about $50 but shuttle transportation to many hotels can be arranged from the terminal. The airport is 26 miles (42 km) from Washington.

7 Baltimore-Washington International Airport

There are five concourses here. A BWI Express Metrobus provides transportation to and from the Greenbelt Metro station. BWI also has its own rail station. Taxis to the city cost about $55. The terminal is 30 miles (48 km) from Washington.

8 By Train

Amtrak provides intercity rail transportation to Washington. The new Acela Express and regional high-speed trains provide shorter travel times, but Metroliners offer less expensive alternatives. Amtrak has a reduced-fare USA Rail Pass for international passengers. Union Station *(see p71)* is the main terminal. ◈ *Amtrak: 800-USA-RAIL/202-484-7540*

9 By Car

Washington has the second worst congestion in the country, which makes driving a less attractive way to get to the city, but larger hotels have parking (about $15 per day), and garages are available. Driving routes to D.C. are I-95 and I-270 from the north, I-66 from the west, I-95 and I-395 from the south, and US 50 from the east.

10 By Bus

The main bus terminals are behind Union Station. Greyhound Lines connect with more than 3,700 locations, and offer low-cost passes. Other bus lines arrive and depart across the street. ◈ *Greyhound: 800-231-2222*

Left **Metrorail sign** Center **Taxi** Right **Road sign**

🔟 Getting Around Washington, D.C.

1 Metrorail
For most destinations in the city, Metrorail, the subway-surface rail system, is the best way to get around. Service is frequent, cars are clean and comfortable, stops are convenient to major sights, and the system is among the safest in the world. Fares depend on distance traveled, ranging from $1.10 to $3.25. There is information on Metrorail's website and the telephone information service. There are 1-day, 7-day, and 28-day passes that allow unlimited trips or a reduced fare.
⊗ *Metrorail: www.wmata. com • Information telephone 202-637-7000 (TDD 202-638-3780) 5:30am–midnight Mon–Thu, 5:30am–2am Fri, 8am–2am Sat, 8am–midnight Sun*

2 Metrobus
The public bus system serves all areas of the city, including destinations not served by Metrorail. Exact change is required – regular routes are $1.10. Vouchers allow passengers to make bus connections within two hours. Information is available from Metrorail.

3 Tour Bus Lines
Tourmobiles are blue-and-white buses that provide an easy way to see major tourist areas. The American Heritage tour, for example, covers 24 stops including Arlington National Cemetery

(see pp30–31). Passengers can disembark and reboard at any stop. The Old Town Trolley provides similar service with 19 stops. ⊗ *Tourmobile: 1000 Ohio Drive SW, www. tourmobile.com, 202-554-5100 • Old Town Trolley: www.trolleytours.com/ Washington.htm, 202-832-9200*

4 Taxis
Washington taxis have a "zone system," with a standard fare from one area to another. Zones are displayed on the back of the driver's seat. A typical trip is $5. Taxis can be hailed on the street, or at stands.

5 Walking
Washington is a city built for walking: sidewalks are wide, intersections have pedestrian walk signs, and drivers are courteous. But scale can be misleading, so wear comfortable shoes.

6 Car Sharing
An innovative hourly car rental program, operated by Metro and Flexcar, can be a boon. Plan members ($25 membership fee) can reserve a car, pick it up at the Metro station nearest their destination, then return it.

7 Rental Cars
Rental car companies are located at all airports, Union Station, and many other locations. The

Yellow Pages will help find the nearest. Renting a car requires a valid driver's license and a major credit card. Drivers must be at least 25 years old. Most cars are automatic, but some companies offer stick-shift controls if requested in advance. ⊗ *Avis: www.avis.com, 800-331-1212 • Budget: www. budgetrentacar.com, 800-527-0700 • Hertz: www. hertz.com, 800-654-3131*

8 Parking
Parking at a car lot will cost $12–$20 per day and about $5 for two hours. Street parking meters have a two-hour maximum, and fines are high. Parking is prohibited on many downtown streets during rush hour, with hours posted on curbside signs. Your car will be towed if you disregard them.

9 Excursions
Transportation to out-of-town attractions such as Mount Vernon *(see pp32–5)* is available from the tour bus lines. Some excursions are also served by rail. Most out-of-town destinations have ample parking.

10 Maps
The Smithsonian Information Center has brochures and maps; hotels and newsstands usually sell maps of the metropolitan area and the rail and bus system.

Left **Visitor Center** Right **Metrobus**

🔟 Sources of Information

1 Washington D.C. Convention and Tourism Corporation

The center for both tourist and business travel to Washington, the organization has an outstanding website and provides information by mail. The site has search capabilities for hotels, shops, restaurants, tourist sights, and transportation. ✆ *Suite 600, 1212 New York Ave, NW • Map P3 • www.washington.org • 202-789-7000*

2 Washington D.C. Visitor Information Center

Advertised as "one-stop shopping" for visitor information, this center comes close to meeting its claim. Its forte is giving advice to walk-in visitors. The center makes hotel reservations with special discounts, and provides information on tourist sights, with inside tips related to the day you are visiting. ✆ *Ronald Reagan International Trade Center Building, 1300 Pennsylvania Ave, NW • www.dcvisit.com • 202-328-4748 • Open 9am-4:30pm Mon - Fri, 9am-4pm Sat (closed Sun)*

3 Metrorail and Metrobus

Hotels generally have metro information and maps, but the metro's website is also excellent *(see p117)*, and system information is displayed in all stations and stops.

4 Smithsonian Institution Information Center

Before you arrive in Washington, the Smithsonian's website is the most convenient source of information. Once in the city, anyone heading for Smithsonian museums or the zoo should visit the Smithsonian Information Center, which also provides interesting displays of its own. ✆ *1000 Jefferson Drive, SW • Map L6 • www.si.edu • 202-357-2700 • Open 9am-5:30pm daily*

5 National Park Service

Many of the sites on the National Mall, especially monuments and memorials, are the responsibility of the National Park Service. Park Service employees will be able to answer most questions. ✆ *900 Ohio Drive, SW • Map N6 • www.nps.gov/nama • 202-619-7225*

6 Washington Post

This internationally respected newspaper is an institution in D.C. As well as news and politics, it is indispensable for its coverage of what's going on in the entertainment and cultural worlds of the city. In it's Friday Weekend tabloid, nearly everything that is current is listed. The *Post's* website (www.washingtonpost. com) is almost as good.

7 Washington City Paper

The *City Paper's* readers are devoted to its coverage of the local music scene and its irreverent look at local culture in general. Available at newsstands and bars and restaurants.

8 Washingtonian Magazine

A city lifestyle magazine, *Washingtonian* provides listings and commentary on cultural institutions and events. It is well known for its coverage of restaurants, featuring the 100 Best. Its website (www.washingtonian. com) has a listing of 100 Best Bargain Restaurants.

9 International Visitors' Information Service

At Dulles International Airport *(see p116)*, foreign-language assistance is available on the lower level at the west end of the concourse near international arrivals. ✆ *International Visitors' Information Service: 703-572-2536/2537*

10 Travelers' Aid Society

Travelers' Aid is located in Union Station *(see p71)* near McDonald's. It provides free advice to travelers needing directions, or for anyone who is stranded in the city. ✆ *Union Station • 202-371-1937 • www.travelersaid. org/ta/dc.htm*

Left **Traffic jam** Right **Reading a street map**

10 Things to Avoid

1 Security Delays and Exclusions

Following the September 2001 terrorist attacks on the United States, security precautions have been strengthened in Washington. Visitors need a government-issued photo ID to enter most government buildings, some office buildings, and even some nightclubs. Visitors to public buildings, including the Smithsonian museums, are prohibited from carrying aerosol and non-aerosol sprays, cans and bottles, food, knives of any sort or other sharp objects such as razors or box-cutters, and mace or pepper spray. Large backpacks are also not allowed, but there is no standard definition of size. Handbags and briefcases will be searched. People have also been delayed or even arrested for remarks officials consider "inappropriate," so don't crack jokes about bombs or weapons.

2 Exhaustion

The openness of the Mall can make distances look shorter than they are. If you start at the Smithsonian metro station, walk to the Lincoln Memorial, to the Capitol, and back to the Metro stop, you will have covered 5 miles (8 km). Whether in D.C.'s humid summer or windy winter, that can be a tiring hike, especially for children.

3 Misinterpreting Washington's Quadrants

The city plan of D.C. arranges all addresses within four quadrants, centered on the dome of the Capitol. Numbered (north-south) and lettered (east-west) streets start on each side of the Capitol. There is a 1st St east of the Capitol and a completely different 1st St west of it. An E St lies north of the Capitol and a different E St south of it. To locate an address, the extension NW, NE, SE, or SW must be noted.

4 Bad Weather

In July and August, temperatures range from about 85°F (30°C) to 95°F (35°C), but the real problem can be humidity. Walk slowly and drink lots of fluids – or visit at some other time of the year. Winters, especially January and February, are windy and raw. Snow and ice storms produce beautiful scenery around the monuments and gardens, but they can paralyze the city temporarily.

5 Street Crime

The greatest protection from street crime is alertness. Thieves depend largely on surprise. Don't carry large amounts of cash or valuables. Keep an accurate record of what's in your wallet, including card numbers and phone numbers of credit card issuers.

6 Dangerous Areas

Tourist zones are safe day and night, but if you want to go to a destination outside these areas, especially at night, ask at your hotel desk for their recommendation.

7 Traffic Jams

Traffic congestion can interfere with plans. Inside the city, traffic moves erratically and slowly. Getting into and out of the city in rush hour (about 6:30–9:30am and 4–7pm) may incur delays of 45 minutes.

8 Discarding Metro Farecard

Metrorail uses a farecard system in which the turnstiles deduct the cost of your trip as you leave the station. You must have a farecard both to enter and to leave, so don't throw it away after getting on the train.

9 Car Break-ins

No matter where you park, don't leave anything in the passenger compartment. If your car radio or CD player is removable, take it with you.

10 Escalator Etiquette

Washington has countless escalators, some of them among the longest in the world. Washingtonians often become angry when the way is blocked – allow people to get past you by standing single-file and to the right.

Left **Union Station shopping mall** Right **Georgetown shops**

Shopping Tips

1 Mall Shopping

If there's one shopping area convenient to Downtown to head for, it would have to be the Fashion Centre at Pentagon City *(see p56)*. The high-quality, high-service Nordstrom's is the anchor store, accompanied by Macy's and over 150 other stores. Name aside, it's not just for fashion. Tysons Corner *(see p57)* is a gigantic complex of two enclosed malls with a huge number and variety of stores and is the most popular shopping destination in the area. It is difficult to reach with public transportation.

2 Georgetown

This has long been an outstanding area for shopping for antiques, fashion, and the unique and unusual *(see p57)*. If you plan to visit Georgetown for shopping, taxi is the best way to get there; the Georgetown metro connection *(see p100)* provides a shuttle from the nearest metro-rail stations, but carrying packages through two transit connections can be tiring.

3 Seasonal Sales and Promotions

No-sales-tax weeks are popular in Washington. Usually two or three weeks before Christmas, these events shave extra percentage points off prices that are often

already reduced. As with everywhere in the US, after-Christmas sales are magnets for shoppers. Sales promotions are common for Presidents' Day in February, July 4th, back-to-school in the last weeks of August, Columbus Day in October, and Veterans' Day in November.

4 Newspaper Specials

Retailers from small shops to huge department stores have sales on special merchandise, overstocks, and regular products to attract customers. The newspapers are the way to find these savings, such as the *Washington Post (see p118)* and the *Washington Times*. Sunday editions, in particular, have many coupons.

5 Sales Tax

The sales tax on general merchandise in Washington is currently 6 percent. In most Virginia jurisdictions, it is 4.5 percent, and in Maryland it is 5 percent.

6 Shopping Hours

Mall and chain stores are usually open from 10am to 9pm Monday to Saturday and noon to 6pm on Sunday. Downtown and independent shops most often operate 10am to 6pm Monday to Saturday. Most shops in Georgetown stay open until 9pm.

7 Museum Shops

The museum shops *(see p83)* have merchandise at all prices. Items costing less than a dollar are lined up next to others costing several hundred dollars or more. Much of the stock in the better museum shops can be purchased nowhere else, so they are well worth a visit.

8 Street Vendors

These have thinned on Washington streets as a result of heightened government security. Interesting, cheap T-shirts are still available, however, along with other souvenir clothing.

9 Yard Sales

Private garage and yard sales are held throughout the city, usually on Saturday or Sunday mornings beginning at 8–9am, and bargains are still to be found. Find listings in the *Washington Post* and the *Washington City Paper (see p118)* or the many online classified advertising sites.

10 Senior Discounts

These popular senior discount shopping days at local department stores are less common than they once were, but they still exist. If you are shopping at a mall or large chain or department store, ask at the information or customer service desk.

  The best website for finding current yard sales in the city is www.washingtoncitypaper.com

ft Washington taxi Center & Right Washington bars

10 Eating and Drinking Tips

1 Alcohol Age Limits

Washington and rrounding jurisdictions, e legal age for purchas-g or drinking alcoholic verages is 21. The law strictly enforced. You ll need a photo ID if u look young enough raise doubt. Many ubs and other venues ow under-21 patrons to ter and enjoy the show, t without a wristband stamped marking, ey are not allowed to y alcohol. It is coming common for ubs and rock concert nues to require photo from everyone, gardless of age.

2 Sales Tax

Tax on restaurant od and on food for mediate consumption 10 percent. Diners with dget concerns should ke this into account, ng with tips. A $20 eal with tax and tip tually costs about $26.

3 Getting Home

The metro closes at dnight during the week d at 2am on Saturday d Sunday mornings, t many clubs, bars, d restaurants stay en later. In most areas ere should be no oblem finding a taxi on e street. Failing that, u can telephone for a xi, but there is a rcharge. If your hotel is the suburbs, the taxi e can be expensive.

4 Microbreweries

Washington is a good place to enjoy unconven-tional and microbrewed beer. Capitol City Brewing Company has a number of locations in the area. Gordon Biersch Brewery Restaurant and John Harvard's Brew House have varieties of hand-made beers. The Brickskeller Saloon-Bar has more than 800 different kinds of beer. ○ Capitol City Brewing Company: 2 Massachusetts Ave, NE • Gordon Biersch Brewery Restaurant: 900 F St, NW • John Harvard's Brew House: 1299 Pennsylvania Ave, NW • The Brickskeller Saloon-Bar: 1523 22nd St, NW

5 Tipping

Restaurant checks rarely include a charge for service. In most restaurants, leaving 15–20 percent of the total charge, including tax, on the table is the common practice. Customers at a bar may leave 10–15 percent of the bar bill or $1 per drink. In a few of the finest restaurants, it is appropriate to tip the maître d' $5 or more if he or she stage-manages the service at your table.

6 Cell Phones

At most restaurants, it is considered bad manners to leave cell phones turned on or to carry on phone conversations inside.

7 Smoking

The trend in the city's restaurants is toward being completely non-smoking. Quite a few restaurants permit smoking in designated areas, especially in parts of town better known for their bars and clubs.

8 Farmers' Markets

For carry-around food and drink, think farmers' markets. These are popular features and often have locally grown fresh produce and other products. There's a year-round Saturday and Sunday market at Eastern Market (see p74) and an April to December seasonal market on Sunday morning at Dupont Circle.

9 Tasting Events

With its embassies, government affairs, and high-powered dinner parties, Washington is a big wine and food city. There are tastings and cooking demonstrations or classes almost every day. Washingtonian Magazine (see p118) keeps an up-to-date registry on its website.

10 Children

If you're traveling with kids and want an all-child-friendly row of easy-to-deal-with restaurants, you can't go wrong in the block of storefronts across from the National Zoo on Connecticut Avenue (see pp28–9).

Left **TicketPlace** discount ticket booth Right **Takeout food outlet**

Tips for Budget Travelers

1 Camping
While there are no campsites or RV campgrounds within the District of Columbia, nearby sites are practical. Cherry Hill Park is served by municipal bus and tourbus lines and is just 3 miles (5 km) from the Greenbelt Metro stop. Capitol KOA runs free shuttle buses to the metro. ○ *Cherry Hill Park: 9800 Cherry Hill Rd, College Park, MD; www.cherryhill park.com; 301-937-7116 • Capitol KOA Campground: 768 Cecil Ave, Millersville, MD; www.koakamp grounds.com/where/md/201 39.htm; 410-923-2771*

2 Discount Tickets
TicketPlace sells half-price theater tickets at its booth at the Old Post Office Pavilion (see p57). Tickets become available on the day of the performance. It is also a Ticketmaster outlet, so regular reservations can be made here. ○ *Ticket-Place: 1100 Pennsylvania Ave, NW • Map P4 • 202-TICKETS • www.cultural -alliance.org/tickets • Open 11am–6pm Tue–Sat*

3 Low Season
Discount hotel rates become available during summer, when Congress is closed, and in the last two weeks in December, and early January. Many hotels offer weekend packages. April through June is the most expensive time to visit.

4 Hotel Discounts
When making reservations at a hotel, ask whether any discounts are available. Many hotels provide discounts for AAA (American Automobile Association) and AARP (American Association of Retired Persons) members. The Visitors' Center (see p118) can book rooms at a discount rate for many hotels.

5 Travel Agents
One resource for finding lower airfares is often neglected today: an experienced travel agent. Fares contracted through a reputable travel agency are almost always lower than those offered by airlines. Similarly, online air reservations can save money. Expedia (www.expedia.com), Travelocity (www. travelocity.com), and Orbitz (www.orbitz.com) are the most popular.

6 Takeout Food
Many smaller hotels that do not have room service or a full-time restaurant will allow patrons to order takeout, delivered to the hotel.

7 Picnics
Delis and produce stores serve every neighborhood. Picnics take finesse in high-security times: if you plan to visit museums or government buildings, you can't carry a knife. Think bite-size items such as cherry

tomatoes and pre-cut cheese, and buy drinks on site. You also can't take food inside, so pla an outdoor spot.

8 Free Entertainment
Take advantage of free entertainment wheneve you can. The film and concert series at the Library of Congress (se pp24–5) are wonderful. The Millennium Stage a the Kennedy Center (se p91) has a great free performance every day. The National Gallery of Art (see pp20–23) also has a concert series, ar the Hirshhorn Museum (see p77) shows movie

9 Cheap Menus
You won't find the traditional $3.99 meatlo dinner in Washington anymore, but *Washing-tonian Magazine*'s "Rea Cheap, Real Good" list a great starting point fo affordable food in pleasant surroundings – entrées for as low as $ in genuinely good restaurants (see p118).

10 Hostels
There is only one hostel in the city, and it is, not surprisingly, in very great demand. Reservations are essential, made as far i advance as possible. ○ *Hostelling International Washington, D.C.: 1009 11th Street, NW • Map P • 202-737-2333 • www. hiwashingtondc.org*

Left **Tourmobile bus** Right **Shopping mall**

10 Tips for Disabled Travelers

1 Metrorail
The metro is fully accessible to disabled travelers. The website (see p117) gives detailed information about accessibility and has a link for out-of-town visitors who will be using the system temporarily. Tactile maps for the system are available at the Columbia Lighthouse for the Blind. Over 70 percent of Metrobus equipment consists of kneeling buses or buses with lifts. ✆ Columbia Lighthouse for the Blind: 202-462-2900

2 Tourmobile
This bus service (see p117) provides access to mobility-restricted passengers, who can transfer from their wheelchairs to priority seating. Wheelchair storage is available. Passengers who need a chair lift can request one at any stop, and a vehicle will be dispatched. Old Town Trolley Tours (see p117) also provide access.

3 Government Buildings
Most have good access for the disabled, but require advance notice for special services such as signed tours. In some instances, accessibility has been lessened due to heightened security measures. The information numbers (see p118) will have current accessibility conditions.

4 Shopping Malls
Most of the newer or recently renovated shopping malls are easily accessible. Union Station (see p71) is notable because it has a metro stop in the building. Other accessible shopping areas in the city limits include the Old Post Office Pavilion, Georgetown Park Mall, and The Shops at National Place (see pp56–7).

5 Access Information Inc
This company publishes the *Access Entertainment Guide* for the Washington, D.C. area. Its website provides reviews of many business and tourist attractions from the point of view of disabled access. It also covers airports, hotels, museums, arenas and concert venues, shops, cinemas, and transportation. ✆ *Access Information Inc: 21618 Slidell Road, Boyds, MD* • www.disabilityguide.com • 301-528-8591

6 Hotels
Nearly all major hotels have some rooms that are wheelchair-accessible. Some have roll-in showers. Other services, such as flashing-light fire alarms, tactile paging, or door-knockers, are widely but not universally available. Information can best be obtained by calling a hotel directly.

7 FDR Memorial
Many places in Washington are welcoming to people with disabilities, but probably none more so than the FDR Memorial (see p82). All four outdoor rooms of this monument are completely accessible. Inscriptions are given in Braille. A sculpture of Franklin D. Roosevelt in his wheelchair has been added to the memorial.

8 National Zoological Park
Washington's Zoo (see pp28–9) has disabled access to nearly all its public areas. The newly refurbished panda environment, for example, is designed with ramps, and viewing angles are calculated to suit the mobility-impaired. Visitors in manual wheelchairs should be warned that the grades on some of the paths are steep.

9 Service Animals
These are allowed anywhere the general public is admitted. It can be convenient to have special harnesses, but these are not required.

10 Smithsonian Information
"Smithsonian Access" is online (www.si.edu/opa/accessibility) and is also available in large-print, audiocassette, Braille, and computer disk at Smithsonian Information (see p118).

All Metro stations are equipped with elevators, but at any given time, some will be out of service for repair or maintenance.

Left **ATM machine** Right **Credit cards**

Banking and Communications

1 ATM Machines
ATM machines are found everywhere in the city, including at the majority of major sights. Cirrus, Plus, and NCYE are the most common networks. Use ATMs to withdraw money during the day in well-populated areas, minimizing the risk of robbery.

2 Banks
You can be almost certain that all banks will be open 9am–2pm Monday to Friday and 9am–noon on Saturday except federal holidays. Some branches have extended hours. Most banks in tourist areas will have the usual services for travelers, including redeeming travelers' checks and currency exchange.

3 Credit Cards
A credit card is essential for car rentals (see p117). Bank debit cards are not accepted for this purpose. Nearly all tourist-related businesses and institutions accept credit cards. It is a good idea to keep a record of the telephone number for reporting credit card thefts.

4 Travelers' Checks
Travelers' checks in US dollars are accepted the same as cash almost everywhere. Restaurants, stores, and tourist sites usually don't even ask for identification, although

banks will often ask for a photo ID. Travelers' checks in foreign currencies can be cashed and exchanged at some, but not all, banks or major hotels, with a valid passport. Keep the proof of purchase separate from the checks.

5 Telephones
The Washington, D.C. area code is 202. Nearby Virginia is 703; Maryland is 301 and 410. Directory assistance from most phones is reached by dialing 411. Cell and wireless coverage is excellent in the immediate area. Using the telephone in your hotel room is the most expensive way to make calls.

6 US Postal Service
Union Station (see p71) and all three airports (see p116) provide postal services for travelers. Blue postal drop boxes are located all over the city. Stamps can be purchased at many hotels, museum and tourist-site gift shops, larger grocery stores, and, of course, post offices. You can find the post office nearest you on the Postal Service website or from their toll-free number. ✆ US Postal Service: www.usps.com, 800-275-8777

7 UPS and Federal Express
Many tourists like to mail home gifts they have bought rather than tote

them in baggage. The Postal Service can be used for this, but United Parcel Service (UPS) and Federal Express have more convenient drop-off locations. It is possible to arrange pickup at most hotels. ✆ UPS: www.ups.com, 800-742-5877
• Federal Express: www.fedex.com, 800-463-3339

8 Internet and Fax
Washington and the surrounding areas are thoroughly wired, but the installation of new fiber-optic cabling explains why many streets are torn up. Most major hotels have fax facilities and provision for connecting to the Internet, either in-room or in a business center. Internet cafés are listed in the Yellow Pages.

9 Currency
The US currency is the dollar, and one dollar is made up of 100 cents. Visitors from outside the US should become familiar with the currency in advance. The new counterfeit-proof bills can be difficult to distinguish from each other.

10 Currency Exchange
Exchange a small amount of currency at the airport and then convert more as needed at city banks where rates are better. Most legal currencies can be exchanged somewhere in Washington.

Left **Police Badge** Center **Fire engine** Right **Hospital Sign**

10 Security and Health

1 Emergency Numbers

Anywhere in or near the city, dialing 911 will summon police, fire, and rescue personnel and equipment as needed. The local 911 system has caller-ID and is able to automatically identify the address from which a call is placed. But this doesn't work as effectively from a cell or wireless phone, so look around for landmarks before you call. You can reach Metro transit police directly at 202-962-2121.

2 Pharmacies

The CVS drugstore chain has a 24-hour pharmacy at Dupont Circle, at 4555 Wisconsin Avenue, NW, and another at 1199 Vermont Avenue NW. Any of these can refer you to pharmacies in other areas.

3 Hospitals and Dentists

Georgetown University Hospital provides a free physician referral service from 9am to 5pm, Monday to Friday. The District of Columbia Dental Society operates a free dental telephone referral service, 8am to 1pm. Most hotels also can make physician and dental referrals.
- *Georgetown University Hospital: 3800 Reservoir Rd NW, Map K2, 202-342-2400*
- *District of Columbia Dental Society: 202-547-7615*

4 Ambulances

An ambulance can be dispatched to emergency health situations by calling 911. Hospital emergency rooms, if you are nearby, are a possible alternative in a crisis, but ambulance crews start stabilizing treatment immediately.

5 Heat Exhaustion

This is a real possibility in summer. Wear light clothing, set a leisurely pace, stay in the shade when possible, and drink plenty of fluids. If you feel very fatigued, light-headed, or weak, get something to drink and sit in the coolest place available. If you don't feel better soon, get medical attention – serious heat exhaustion can be life-threatening.

6 Driving

Drivers and all car passengers, front and back, are required to wear seat belts. Children under three years old must be seated in a child-restraint seat. Laws against drinking and driving are very strictly enforced by the police.

7 Pedestrian Crossings

Washington drivers are not as hazardous as those in some cities. The biggest exception is running red lights. Make certain that opposing traffic has stopped before you venture into the crosswalk.

8 Escalators

Washington is a city of escalators, and there have been a surprising number of deaths and injuries. Use the handrail, and keep loose clothing and shoelaces away from moving parts at the sides and bottom and top of the escalator. Use an elevator if you have children in a stroller or are carrying heavy luggage.

9 Metrorail

The system can be very crowded during rush hour. Especially if you are traveling with children, be certain to keep your party together. Locals generally have a plan for what to do if a child ends up on the train and the parents don't, or vice versa. The usual drill is for the child to get off the train at the next stop and wait for the parents to arrive. If it's the child that doesn't get on, he or she waits for the parents to backtrack to the station.

10 Boating

A number of rental services provide equipment for boating on the Potomac. This can be great fun, but the Potomac is dangerous. Follow all safety rules, and be certain to use the safety vests provided. The Great Falls area *(see p108)* is extremely hazardous. People die every year after falling from the treacherous rocks here.

Left **Willard Inter-Continental** Right **Jefferson Hotel**

🔟 Historic Hotels

1 Willard Inter-Continental

This is certainly among the most historic of hotels. Epochal events, including the birth of the League of Nations, were discussed here by principal figures. Royalty from all over the world have been guests *(see p88).* ⓢ *1401 Pennsylvania Ave, NW • Map P4 • 202-628-9100 • washington. interconti.com • Dis. access • $$$$$*

2 Hay-Adams Hotel

Constructed on the sites of the homes of John Hay and Henry Adams, this elegant hotel has carried on the tradition of the finest hospitality. The recent restoration is a triumph. ⓢ *16th and H Sts, NW • Map N3 • 202-638-6600 • www.hayadams.com • Dis. access • $$$$$*

3 Renaissance Mayflower Hotel

Opened to a huge crowd on the day of Calvin Coolidge's 1925 presidential inauguration, this hotel has been a fixture for politicians – Franklin D. Roosevelt wrote his 1933 inaugural address here and J. Edgar Hoover had lunch here nearly every day. A classic hotel with complimentary shoe shines, and multilingual staff. ⓢ *1127 Connecticut Ave, NW • Map N3 • 202-347-3000 • www. renaissancehotels.com • Dis. access • $$$$*

4 Jefferson Hotel

The decorations on the Beaux Arts façade are eye-catchers, and inside are displayed prints and documents, including some associated with Thomas Jefferson. The hotel is popular with celebrities. It has in-room VCRs and CD players. ⓢ *16th & M Sts, NW • Map N2 • 202-347-2200 • www.loewshotels.com • Dis. access • $$–$$$$*

5 St. Regis Hotel

If both Queen Elizabeth II and the Rolling Stones chose to stay here, the St. Regis must be doing something right. Calvin Coolidge took part in the 1926 opening of this grand hotel, styled after a Renaissance palace and appointed with antiques, chandeliers, and fine tapestries. ⓢ *923 16th St, NW • Map N2 • 202-638-2626 • www.stregis.com • Dis. access • $$$–$$$$*

6 Hotel Washington

For 80 years, diplomats, politicians, and celebrities have visited the Hotel Washington, seeking its prime location next to the White House and its exceptional service. Many rooms have views of the White House or Capitol, and the top-floor restaurant offers superb panoramic vistas. ⓢ *515 15th Street, NW • Map P4 • 202-638-5900 • www.hotelwashington. com • Dis. access • $$$*

7 Morrison-Clark Inn

Created from two townhouses, this mansion served as the Soldiers, Sailors, Marines, and Airmen's Club for nearly 50 years. Decorative touches remain, including four gorgeous tall mirrors ⓢ *1101 L St, NW • Map P3 • 202-898-1200 • www. morrisonclark.com • $$$*

8 Phoenix Park Hotel

Named after the famous park in Dublin, this hotel expresses an understated Irish theme. The stately Georgian Revival hotel, built in 1922, retain an Old World flavor. ⓢ *520 N Capitol St, NW • Map R4 • 202-638-6900 • www.phoenixparkhotel. com • Dis. access • $$$*

9 Henley Park Hotel

The outside is festooned with gargoyles, and the interior boasts original stained glass. Four-poster beds furnish some rooms. ⓢ *926 Massachusetts Ave, NW • Map Q3 • 202-638-5200 • www.cchotels.com • Dis. access • $$$*

10 Churchill Hotel

Opened as an apartment building in 1906, this grand hotel provides huge, tastefully furnished rooms with panoramic views. ⓢ *1914 Connecticu Ave, NW • Map N2 • 202-797-2000 • www. thechurchillhotel.com • Dis. access • $$$*

Note: Unless otherwise stated, all hotels accept credit cards, and have en-suite bathrooms and air conditioning

Price Categories

For a standard, double room per night (with breakfast if included), taxes and extra charges.

$	under $100
$$	$100–$200
$$$	$200–$350
$$$$	$350–$500
$$$$$	over $500

Above **Lobby, Washington Court**

Luxury Hotels

1 Grand Hyatt Washington

The location is superb and the concierge offers full information on local sports, theaters, and events, and can arrange to have a rental bicycle delivered. The sports bar is a popular meeting place, and the business center even offers desktop publishing. ◎ *1000 H St, NW • Map P3 • 202-582-1234 • www. washingtongrand.hyatt.com • Dis. access • $$$*

2 Four Seasons Hotel

A high-profile hotel for high-profile travelers. The spa is renowned, and afternoon tea at the Garden Terrace will make any visitor feel special. Convenient to Georgetown and Rock Creek Park. ◎ *2800 Pennsylvania Ave, NW • Map L3 • 202-342-0444 • www.four seasons.com/washington • Dis. access • $$$$*

3 Hilton and Towers Washington

The garden setting is lovely, and the elevated location gives a good view of the skyline. Both the layout and size of this complex create a resort atmosphere, while staff and facilities offer every amenity. The Olympic-sized pool is an attraction in the summer. ◎ *1919 Connecticut Ave, NW • Map N1 • 202-483-3000 • www.washingtonhilton.com • Dis. access • $$$*

4 Park Hyatt Washington

The decor at this refurbished hotel features original artwork. Indoor pool, a sauna, and steam room. The Melrose Restaurant *(see p63)* is among the best in the city. ◎ *24th St at M St, NW • Map M2 • 202-789-1234 • parkwashington.hyatt.com • Dis. access • $$$*

5 The Watergate Hotel

Rooms are large with separate seating areas, and often a balcony. A full health club, a beauty salon, and an indoor pool and sauna are provided. All rooms have Internet access, voice mail, and fax. The location on the Potomac is hard to beat. ◎ *2650 Virginia Ave, NW • Map M3 • 202-965-2300 • www.thewatergate.com • $$–$$$$$*

6 Ritz-Carlton

The Ritz-Carlton provides the finest quality furnishings – Egyptian cotton sheets and down pillows – to make guests comfortable. The marble bathrooms are roomy. Internet access provided in all rooms. ◎ *1150 22nd St, NW • Map M3 • 202-835-0500 • www.ritzcarlton. com • Dis. access • $$$$*

7 Westin Embassy Row

The theme here is country elegance, reflected in the decor. Located at a prime Embassy Row location, the hotel attracts diplomats, and also celebrities looking for less conspicuous accommodations. A concierge and a fitness room are available 24 hours a day. ◎ *2100 Massachusetts Ave, NW • Map M2 • 202-293-2100 • www.westin.com • Dis. access • $$$*

8 Monarch Hotel

This hotel's garden courtyard is gorgeous, and a recent $12 million renovation has made the entire hotel a showplace. Some rooms have delightful balconies. ◎ *2401 M St, NW • Map M2 • 202-429-2400 • www.monarchdc.com • Dis. access • $$$*

9 Hyatt Regency Washington on Capitol Hill

A bustling hotel that takes up an entire block. The rooftop restaurant overlooks the Capitol – dazzling at night. ◎ *400 New Jersey Ave, NW • Map R4 • 202-737-1234 • www.hyatt.com • Dis. access • $$$*

10 Washington Court Hotel

Larger than average rooms and the location is convenient. The lobby is an atrium design with a waterfall. ◎ *525 New Jersey Ave, NW • Map R4 • 202-628-2100 • www. washingtoncourthotel.com • Dis. access • $$$*

Left and Right **Latham Hotel**

TOP10 Moderately Priced Hotels

1 Latham Hotel
Best known locally as the home of the top-rated Citronelle restaurant *(see p105)*, this is a fine hotel in an excellent Georgetown location. Distinctive two-story carriage suites are available, providing a gracious home base for visiting the area. The poolside patio overlooks the C&O Canal. ✪ *3000 M St, NW • Map L2 • 202-726-5000 • www.thelatham.com • $$*

2 Jury's Normandy Inn
On a quiet residential street, the Normandy has the feel of a bed-and-breakfast. Complimentary wine and cheese are served Tuesday nights, and coffee, tea, and cookies are offered at other times. ✪ *2118 Wyoming Ave, NW • Map J5 • 202-483-1350 • $$*

3 Capitol Hill Suites
This suites-only hotel was recreated from an apartment building, and the result is large spaces with kitchens or kitchenettes. Near the Library of Congress, the US Capitol, and Eastern Market. ✪ *200 C St, SE • Map S5 • 202-543-6000 • $$*

4 Georgetown Inn
This hotel opened in 1961 at the height of the Kennedy administration and the interest in Georgetown glamour, and it has been a fixture ever since. The rooms

are large and decorated with style. The Executive Rooms have a sitting area large enough for a meeting, and all rooms have high-speed Internet access. ✪ *1310 Wisconsin Ave, NW • Map L2 • 202-333-8900 • www.georgetowninn.com • $$–$$$*

5 Best Western New Hampshire Suites
This is a good downtown version of the motel chain, small and relatively quiet, given its popularity with families. The lobby has a working fireplace. All rooms are suites with a separate sitting area and kitchenette. Continental breakfast is included. ✪ *1121 New Hampshire Ave, NW • Map M3 • 202-457-0565 • www.bestwestern.com • Dis. access • $$*

6 Marriott at Metro Center
An excellent downtown location, close to the Mall. This big hotel, with 465 rooms, still provides a personal touch. The Regatta Raw Bar has seasonal food. ✪ *775 12th St, NW • Map P3 • 202-737-2200 • www.marriotthotels.com • Dis. access • $$–$$$*

7 Holiday Inn on the Hill
The well-known chain has recently refurbished this Capitol Hill location, adding features that appeal to both business

travelers and families. The fitness center is open 24 hours, and some rooms offer Internet access. Special activities and services are offered for children. ✪ *415 New Jersey Ave, NW • Map R4 • 202-638-1616 • www.holiday-inn.com/was-onthehill • Dis. access • $$*

8 Georgetown Suites
One of two similar hotels under the same management, Georgetown Suites offers a range of lodging possibilities, all of which have a separate sitting area and a kitchen. ✪ *1000 29th St, NW • Map L3 • 202-298-7800 • www.georgetownsuites.com • Dis. access • $$*

9 Renaissance Hotel Washington, D.C.
This big hotel – over 800 rooms and 500 more being added – is hard to miss with its striking façade. Oriented toward business travelers, but still a good location for families. ✪ *999 9th St, NW • Map Q3 • 202-898-9000 • www.renaissancehotel.com • Dis. access • $$–$$$*

10 Radisson Barceló Hotel
The rooms are very large in this converted apartment building. The lively Gabriel restaurant offers Mediterranean and Latin American dishes. ✪ *2121 P St, NW • Map M2 • 202-293-3100 • www.radisson.com • $$–$$$*

Note: Unless otherwise stated, all hotels accept credit cards, and have en-suite bathrooms and air conditioning

Price Categories

For a standard, double room per night (with breakfast if included), taxes and extra charges.

$	under $100
$$	$100–$200
$$$	$200–$350
$$$$	$350–$500
$$$$$	over $500

Above **Braxton Hotel**

Budget Hotels

1 Braxton Hotel
This charming old building, about six blocks from the White House, has been converted into 62 rooms that are popular with young people on a limited budget. Some rooms have little refrigerators or microwaves. ☜ 1440 Rhode Island Ave, NW • Map P2 • 202-232-7800 • www.braxtonhotel.com • $–$$

2 Swiss Inn
The smallest hotel in downtown Washington, and rightly proud of it. The size – 21 rooms – allows more personal attention to guests. Comfortable rooms have TVs and a kitchenette. There is a flower garden in front of the hotel. ☜ 1204 Massachusetts Ave, NW • Map P3 • 202-371-1816 • www.theswissinn.com • $

3 Adams Inn
A European-style small hotel, with 27 rooms. The hotel spreads over three 100-year-old townhouses. Convenient to Adams Morgan and the Zoo. Many rooms share a bath but have a sink in the room. ☜ 1744 Lanier Place, NW • Map J4 • 202-745-3600 • www.adamsinn.com • $

4 Kalorama Guest House
Spanning a number of architecturally significant townhouses, the Guest House provides a comfortable base in an unbeatable neighborhood. The well-maintained rooms are handsomely furnished with plants, Oriental carpets, and period artwork. Continental breakfast included. ☜ 1854 Mintwood Place, NW • Map M1 • 202-667-6369 • $

5 Embassy Inn
An elegant apartment house built in 1910 has been converted into a small hotel with 38 guest rooms, all with private bath. Much of the original decor remains, and the tasteful façade and entranceway are worthy of Paris. Cable TV and direct-dial telephones serve every room. Continental breakfast included. ☜ 1627 16th St, NW • Map N2 • 202-234-7800 • Dis. access • $–$$

6 Allen Lee Hotel
A gracious and simple home base for exploring the city and a terrific bargain. Located near George Washington University. All rooms have telephone and TV. ☜ 2224 F St, NW • Map M4 • 202-331-1224 • www.allenleehotel.com • $

7 The River Inn
This popular Foggy Bottom hotel has 126 suites, each with a full kitchen and a good-sized work or dining area. The name is apt because the remarkable view of the river is bound to put guests in a good mood after a tiring day of sightseeing. ☜ 924 25th St, NW • Map M3 • 202-337-7600 • www.theriverinn.com • Dis. access • $$

8 Brickskeller Inn
Basic accommodations in a nice area west of Dupont Circle. Convenient to many good restaurants and to Rock Creek Park. The Brickskeller Saloon-Bar (see p62) is the real attraction here. ☜ 1523 22nd St, NW • Map M2 • 202-293-1885 • Dis. access • $

9 Hotel Harrington
At one time, this was the largest hotel in Washington, and it is still operated by members of the founding family, a century later. Not expensive and popular with school groups. Has outstanding family suites with two bathrooms. ☜ 11th & E Sts, NW • Map P4 • 202-628-8140 • www.hotel-harrington.com • $$

10 Channel Inn
This hotel is directly on the Southwest Waterfront, with a great view of Washington Channel and Haines Point and a five-minute walk to the Fish Wharf. The bedrooms have an English-country look, and each has a small balcony – a joy in good weather. ☜ 650 Water St, SW • Map Q6 • 202-554-2400 • www.channelinn.com • Dis. access • $$

Left **Loew's L'Enfant Plaza Hotel** Right **Swimming pool, Washington Plaza**

Child-Friendly Hotels

1 Holiday Inn Capitol at the Smithsonian

Outdoor rooftop pool with a view, kids eat free, one block from the Air and Space Museum – this combination is hard to beat. The on-site deli provides quick meals and snacks, and there are guest laundry facilities. ✪ *550 C St, SW • Map Q5 • 202-479-4000 • www. holiday-inn.com • Dis. access • $$*

2 Loew's L'Enfant Plaza Hotel

The Mall is an easy two-block walk from here, and when visitors are not exploring Smithsonian museums, they can enjoy the amenities and fine river views here. Special treats for children include a small gift, a free movie with popcorn, little TVs in the bathrooms, and indoor pool. ✪ *480 L'Enfant Plaza SW • Map Q5 • 202-484-1000 • www. loewshotels.com • Dis. access • $$$*

3 Red Roof Inn, Washington DC Downtown

All the friendly Red Roof family extras: kids can rent video games for in-room play; the TV cable service includes the Cartoon, Discovery, and Learning channels; snack centers relieve the munchies. ✪ *500 H St, NW • Map Q3 • 202-289-5959 • www.redroof.com • Dis. access • $$*

4 Washington Plaza

The beautifully landscaped and resort-like hotel surrounds the big outdoor pool. In warm weather, poolside barbecues are offered on Friday nights. ✪ *10 Thomas Circle, NW • Map P3 • 202-842-1300 • www.cchotels.com • Dis. access • $$–$$$*

5 J.W. Marriott

Two blocks from the White House, the location minimizes walking distances for little feet. Child care is offered. ✪ *1331 Pennsylvania Ave, NW • Map P4 • 202-393-2000 • www.marriotthotels.com • Dis. access • $$$$*

6 Washington Courtyard Marriott/Northwest

Convenient to the National Zoo (*see pp28–9*), this hotel provides extra guest-room space and good services. The outdoor pool is safe and fun. Free cookies in the lobby every afternoon. ✪ *1900 Connecticut Ave NW • Map N1 • 202-332-9300 • www.marriott.com • Dis. access • $$$*

7 Holiday Inn Central

This downtown hotel has recently added in-room Nintendo game consoles, which, added to the rooftop pool and cable TV and in-room movies, make a pretty complete package for children.

Some oversized rooms available. Both Dupont Circle and McPherson Square Metro stops are within walking distance. *Rhode Island Ave at 15th St, NW • Map P2 • 202-483-2000 • www.inn-dc.com • Dis. access • $$*

8 Lincoln Suites

The whimsical decorations will appeal to urban-oriented kids. In-room movies and pay-to-play Nintendo are offered. ✪ *1823 L St, NW • Map N3 • 202-223-4320 • www.lincolnhotels.com • Dis. access • $$*

9 Washington Suites Georgetown

This excellent George-town location provides separate living rooms, two TVs, and a fully equipped kitchen including a dishwasher. . Pets allowed. ✪ *2500 Pennsylvania Ave, NW • Map M3 • 202-333-8060 • www.washingtonsuites. com • Dis. access • $$–$$$*

10 Hilton Arlington and Towers

Outside the city center, located directly at the Ballston Metro Center. Suburban shopping and activities are convenient by car from here. ✪ *950 N Stafford St, Arlington, VA • Map C4 • 703-528-6000 • www.hilton.com • Dis. access • $$$*

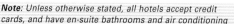

Note: *Unless otherwise stated, all hotels accept credit cards, and have en-suite bathrooms and air conditioning*

Price Categories

For a standard, double room per night (with breakfast if included), taxes and extra charges.

$	under $100
$$	$100–$200
$$$	$200–$350
$$$$	$350–$500
$$$$$	over $500

Above **The Inn at Dupont Circle**

Bed-and-Breakfasts

1 Bed-and-Breakfast Accommodations

A booking agency specializing in B&Bs in and around the city. It lists some of the most attractive properties. Staff personally inspect guesthouses on a regular basis. ✆ *PO Box 12011, Washington, DC 20005 • 877-893-3233 (Toll free), 202-328-3510 • www. bnbaccom.com.*

2 The Inn at Dupont Circle

This beautiful little inn is one block from Dupont Circle, and its guests partake of the myriad of restaurants, shops, movie theaters, and art galleries in the neighborhood. The interesting building, with high ceilings and a walled garden, dates from 1855 and once was owned by astrologer Jeanne Dixon. ✆ *1312 19th St, NW • Map N2 • 202-467-6777 • www. theinnatdupontcircle.com • $$*

3 Mansion on O Street

Lavishly decorated, this inn offers a variety of themed rooms, including a two-story log cabin motif and several Art Deco stylings. The layout is so striking that guests often treat the house as a sight in itself. Rooms have up-to-date business services with private phone lines. ✆ *2020 O St, NW • Map N2 • 202-496-2000 • www.erols. com/mansion • $$$*

4 Hereford House

In a Capitol Hill residential neighborhood, one block from the metro, this Federal-style townhouse provides a true B&B experience. There are no in-room TVs or telephones. The breakfasts are exceptional, including a changing menu of cooked treats. ✆ *604 S Carolina Ave, SE • Map S5 • 202-543-0102 • $*

5 Bull Moose Bed & Breakfast

A handsome three-story Victorian rowhouse, the interior finish, including the woodwork and stairway, are original. The rooms are inviting and stylishly furnished. ✆ *101 5th St, NE • Map S4 • 202-547-1050 • www.guesthse. com/caphill • $$*

6 Swann House

Sometimes described as the best B&B in the city, this charming establishment provides modern conveniences along with personal attention. All rooms have private baths and cable TV. ✆ *1808 New Hampshire Ave, NW • Map N1 • 202-265-4414 • www. swannhouse.com • $$–$$$*

7 Aaron Shipman House

This classic Victorian mansion, lovingly restored and maintained, is well furnished and decorated. Famous for its Christmas decorations. Breakfast – far more elaborate than just "continental" – is served in an elegant dining room. ✆ *Q St, NW near 13th St • Map P2 • 877-893-3233 (Toll free), 202-328-3510 • www.aaron shipmanhouse.com • $$*

8 MacMillan House

Out of the city center but convenient for longer-term visitors because of reasonable weekly and monthly rates, MacMillan House is a completely renovated townhouse from the early 20th century. Guest rooms are large and comfortable. Off-street parking. Multi-room suites available. ✆ *1032 Perry St, NE • Map D3 • 202-636-9399 • $$*

9 Aiko's Bed & Breakfast

Hosted by Aiko Ichimura, this captivating B&B is warmly furnished with Japanese influences. Breakfast is an occasion. TV/VCR provided. ✆ *1411 Hopkins St, NW (between O and P Sts, NW) • Map P2 • 202-293-3039 • www. users.erols.com/aikop • $$*

10 Apartment on the Hill

An apartment in a private house rented to visitors. Breakfast is self-catered, with high-quality, fresh ingredients provided by the hosts. Pleasingly decorated and furnished in English-country style. ✆ *603 Massachusetts Ave NE • Map S4 • 202-547-5969 • www.apartment onthehill.com • $$*

Left and Right **The Hotel George**

TOP 10 Boutique Hotels

1 Topaz

The striking interiors here are in the highest contemporary style, with exquisite design. The Topaz Bar is among the best in the city, and hotel services include a daily horoscope. ◎ *1733 N St, NW • Map N2 • 202-393-3000 • www.topazhotel. com • $$$*

2 Hotel George

One of the most fashionable hotels in the city, deserving attention because of its innovative design, excellent business accommodations (the desks are huge slices of granite with contemporary communications), and its fine bistro-style restaurant. The in-room CD player/ radio provides sound environments including ocean, brook, forest, or wind. ◎ *15 E St, NW • Map R4 • 202-347-4200 • www.hotelgeorge.com • Dis. access • $$$*

3 Sofitel Lafayette Square

On a corner of Lafayette Square, this 1862 building has been transformed by the French Sofitel chain into an elegant contemporary hotel. The soundproofing and acoustic doors are a welcome feature. The restaurant serves refined French cuisine. ◎ *806 15th St, NW • Map P4 • 202-737-8800 • www. sofitel.com • Dis. access • $$$$*

4 George Washington University Inn

The handsome and large guest rooms and suites are colonial-inspired, but all have a refrigerator, microwave, and coffee-maker. Some have complete kitchens. The Kennedy Center is nearby. ◎ *824 New Hampshire Ave, NW • Map M3 • 202-337-6620 • www.gwuinn.com • Dis. access • $$$*

5 Hotel Monticello

Mini-suites with refrigerator, microwave, and coffee service are offered at this elegant hotel at one of the best addresses, right up from the C&O canal in Georgetown. The fixtures are beautiful – marble bathrooms and good art on the walls. The staff emphasizes personal attention to guests' needs. ◎ *1075 Thomas Jefferson St, NW • Map L3 • 202-337-0900 • www. hotelmonticello.com • $$$*

6 Windsor Inn

Two 1920s buildings offer big hotel amenities in a charming and personable environment. The main building is on the National Register of Historic Places, and has some marvelous Art Deco ornamentation. Evening sherry in the lounge. No elevator. ◎ *1842 16th St, NW • Map N1 • 202-667-0300 • $$*

7 Hotel Lombardy

A recent refurbishing transformed this hotel with imported fabrics, Oriental rugs, and original art. The restaurant is bistro-style. ◎ *2019 Pennsylvania Ave, NW • Map N3 • 202-828-2600 • www.hotellombardy.com • $$$*

8 Hotel Madera

Newly renovated, this small hotel exudes elegance, sophistication, and power, catering to ladies and gentlemen of classical tastes. ◎ *1310 New Hampshire Ave, NW • Map N2 • 202-296-7600 • www.hotelmadera.com • $$$*

9 Madison Hotel

Billing itself as "Washington's Correct Address," this hotel is filled with the finest of everything. The decorative items and artwork displayed throughout the hotel are of collector's quality. ◎ *1157 15th at M St, NW • Map P2 • 202-862-1600 • www. themadisonhotel.net • $$$*

10 Melrose Hotel

A modern building in a first-rate location at the heart of the city, the Melrose is well known for its refined luxury. The furnishings are contemporary but with classic influences. ◎ *2430 Pennsylvania Ave, NW • Map M3 • www.melrosehotel.com • Dis. access • $$$$*

  Note: *Unless otherwise stated, all hotels accept credit cards, and have en-suite bathrooms and air conditioning*

Price Categories	
For a standard,	**$** under $100
double room per	**$$** $100–$200
night (with breakfast	**$$$** $200–$350
if included), taxes	**$$$$** $350–$500
and extra charges.	**$$$$$** over $500

Above **Typical Washington, D.C. business hotel lobby**

10 Business Hotels

1 Marriott Wardman Park
The largest convention hotel in Washington combines charm with modern services and technology. There are scores of meeting rooms here and an exhibition area. The well-maintained rooms offer all business services. ⊗ *2660 Woodley Rd, NW • Map J5 • 202-328-2000 • www.marriott.com • Dis. access $$$–$$$$$*

2 Crystal City Marriott
This hotel has all business amenities and is convenient to the Pentagon and within a mile of Ronald Reagan Airport. There are 13 meeting rooms, a concierge, and a business center. ⊗ *1999 Jefferson Davis Highway, Arlington VA • Map D4 • 703-413-5500 • www.marriotthotels.com • Dis. access • $$–$$$*

3 Omni Shoreham Hotel
Adjacent to Rock Creek Park, this grand hotel sits on 11 landscaped acres. A dynamic, luxury hotel that has hosted countless important guests and meetings. The full business center also includes clerical support. Multiple large meeting rooms. ⊗ *2500 Calvert St, NW (near Connecticut Ave) • Map J5 • 202-234-0700 • www. omnihotels.com • Dis. access • $$$*

4 Hamilton Crowne Plaza Hotel
This distinguished hotel has recently been renovated. The guest rooms offer a desk with a modem connection and voice mail, and cable TV with in-room movies. Fourteen meeting rooms are available with teleconferencing and a multilingual staff. ⊗ *1001 14th at K St, NW • Map P3 • 202-682-0111 • www. crowneplazawashington.com • $$$*

5 Embassy Suites Hotel Downtown
Well-furnished rooms with good work areas and a separate living room for meetings or relaxing. Conference rooms with extensive equipment available for rent. Indoor swimming pool and fitness center. Breakfast included. ⊗ *1250 22nd St, NW • Map M3 • 202-857-3388 • www.embassysuites dcmetro.com/downtown • Dis. access • $$$*

6 One Washington Circle
Business travelers receive excellent services at this Foggy Bottom hotel. A knowledgable staff manages the four meeting rooms, and suites have lots of seating space for work. Larger suites have full kitchens. ⊗ *1 Washington Circle, NW • Map N3 • 202-872-1680 • www.Hwcirclehotel.com • $$$*

7 Capital Hilton
A huge range of meeting rooms and guest rooms with desks and modern communications. ⊗ *1001 K St at 16th St. NW • Map N3 • 202-393-1000 • www.capital.hilton.com • Dis. access • $$$$*

8 Four Points by Sheraton
Totally remade from a motel-like facility into a very modern business hotel with professional meeting specialist. The garden terrace around the indoor pool can be booked for functions. ⊗ *1201 K St, NW • Map P3 • 202-289-7600 • www. fourpointswashingtondc.com • Dis. access • $$–$$$*

9 Best Western Downtown/ Capitol Hill
Convenient to the Capitol with good business services. The meeting facilities are small but well maintained. ⊗ *724 3rd St, NW • Map R4 • 202-842-4466 • www. bestwestern.com • Dis. access • $$*

10 Courtyard by Marriott Convention Center
Situated in an old 1891 bank but completely up-to-date. Near both of the city's convention centers. Four conference rooms. ⊗ *900 F St NW • Map Q4 • 202-638-4600 • www.courtyard.com • Dis. access • $$$*

General Index

Acknowledgments

Main Contributors
Ron Burke is the author or co-author of 19 books. A former Capitol Hill resident, he was born in the Washington, D.C. metropolitan area and has lived here most of his life.

Susan Burke lives in Virginia, where she worked on a daily newspaper for 20 years before becoming an editor for the Air Line Pilots Association. She is also a freelance editor for journals on labor, economics, and art conservation.

Produced by Sargasso Media Ltd, London

Project Editor Zoë Ross
Art Editor Philip Lord
Picture Research Helen Stallion
Proofreader Stewart J Wild
Indexer Hilary Bird
Editorial Assistance Ebba Tinwin

Main Photographer Scott Suchman

Additional Photography
Phillipe Dewet, Kim Sayer, Giles Stokoe

Illustrator chrisorr.com

FOR DORLING KINDERSLEY
Publishing Manager Marisa Renzullo
Publisher Douglas Amrine
Senior Cartographic Editor Casper Morris
Senior DTP Jason Little
Production Melanie Dowland
Picture Librarians Hayley Smith, David Saldanha

Maps John Plumer

Additional Contributors
Sherry Collins, Esther Labi, Litta W. Sanderson

Picture Credits
t-top, tl-top left; tlc-top left center; tc-top center; tr-top right; cla-center left above; ca-center above; cra-center right above; cl-center left; c-center; cr-center right; clb-center left below; cb-center below; crb-center right below; bl-bottom left, b-bottom; bc-bottom center; bcl-bottom center left; br-bottom right; d-detail.

Every effort has been made to trace the copyright holders of images, and we apologize in advance for any unintentional omissions. We would be pleased to insert the appropriate acknowledgements in any subsequent edition of this publication.

The publishers would like to thank the following individuals, companies and picture libraries for their kind permission to reproduce their photographs:

Abbie Row/National Park Service: 15; Allsport: 61r; Astorino PhotoGraphics Inc. Alexandria, Virginia: 83tl

Christine Parker, Courtesy of the Heritage Smithsonian Institution: 64b; Corbis: 4–5, 6t, 8b, 8–9, 10tl, 10tr, 10b, 32t, 36tl, 36tr, 36c, 36b, 37l, 37r, 38tl, 38tr, 38c, 38b, 39l,

39tr, 39br, 54tl, 55r, 65r, 80–81, 96tr, 102–103, 106tl, 110–11, 114–15; Courtesy of the Heritage Smithsonian Institution: 64tl; Courtesy of the Mount Vernon Ladies' Association: 7t, 32bl, 32br, 32–3, 33c, 64tl

Library of Congress: 25t; Eric Long/Smithsonian Institution: 83tr

National Air and Space Museum: 16c, 17ca; National Cherry Blossom Festival: 64tr; National Gallery of Art, Washington: Fra Angelico & Filippo Lippi, *The Adoration of the Magi*, c1445, Samuel H. Kress Collection: 20b; Alexander Calder, *Cheval Rouge (Red Horse)* 1974, Courtesy of the Calder Foundation, (c) ARS, NY & DACS, London 2002: 23b, John Constable, *Wivenhoe Park*, 1816, Widener Collection: 21t; Leonardo da Vinci, *Ginevra de Benci*, Ailsa Mellon Bruce Fund: 20cl; Frans Hals, *Portrait of an Elderly Lady*, 1633, Andrew W. Mellon Collection: 22b; Claude Monet, *The Japanese Footbridge*, 1899, Gift of Victorian Mebeker Coberly, in memory of her son John W. Mudd, and Walter H. and Leonore Annenburg: 22tc; Maurice Brazil Prendegast, *Salem Cove*, 1916, Collection of Mr and Mrs Paul Mellon: 22tl; Gilbert Stuart, *George Washington*, c1821, Gift of Thomas Jefferson Coolidge V, in Memory of his Great Grandfather, Thomas Jefferson Coolidge, His Grandfather, Thomas Jefferson Coolidge II and his Father, Thomas Jefferson Coolidge III: 7cl, 21b; Johannes Vermeer, *Girl with the Red Hat*, Andrew W. Mellon Collection: 20cr; James McNeill Whistler, *The White Girl*, 1862, Harris Whittmore Collections: 21c; National Museum of American History: 6br, 18c, 18b, 19t, 19c, 19b; Northwest Flower and Garden Show: 65tl

Smithsonian National Zoological Park/Jessie Cohen: 7cr, 28t, 28bl, 28-29, 29t, 29cr, 29cl

US Capitol Historical Society: 9cr, 9b

Veridian Systems Division: 17cb;

White House Collection, Courtesy White House Historical Trust: 6bl, 12b, 12–13, 13t, 13cb, 13b, 14tl, 14tr, 14b.

Front Cover:
CORBIS, Richard T. Nowitz tc; DK PICTURE LIBRARY, Kim Sayer – main image, cla, clb; Mae Scanlan b.
Back Cover:
DK PICTURE LIBRARY Kim Sayer tl, tc, tr; Washington Metropolitan Area Transit Authority: inside back

Selected Street Index